AGENT *YOU*

NICOLE LYNN

FOREWORD BY GABRIELLE UNION

AGENT *YOU*

Show Up, Do the Work, and Succeed on Your Own Terms

HARPER HORIZON

Dedicated to every woman who is
making room for other women at the table

Published by Harper Horizon, an imprint of HarperCollins Focus LLC.

Any internet addresses, phone numbers, or company or product information printed in this book are offered as a resource and are not intended in any way to be or to imply an endorsement by Harper Horizon, nor does Harper Horizon vouch for the existence, content, or services of these sites, phone numbers, companies, or products beyond the life of this book.

Scripture quotations are taken from the Holy Bible, New International Version®, NIV®. Copyright © 1973, 1978, 1984, 2011 by Biblica, Inc.® Used by permission of Zondervan. All rights reserved worldwide. www .zondervan.com. The "NIV" and "New International Version" are trademarks registered in the United States Patent and Trademark Office by Biblica, Inc.®

ISBN 978-0-7852-3805-8 (eBook)
ISBN 978-0-7852-3804-1 (HC)

Library of Congress Control Number: 2021930956

Printed in the United States of America
21 22 23 24 25 LSC 10 9 8 7 6 5 4 3 2 1

CONTENTS

FOREWORD

Nicole Lynn is a woman after my own heart—brave, passionate, insanely hardworking. She lives life to the fullest and won't stop until she gets all that she came for. Making history as the first black female sports agent to land a top 3 NFL draft pick, Nicole Lynn shattered the glass ceiling and is a rising icon and an unstoppable megaforce behind some of sports' biggest names.

Though Nicole and I work in different fields, we share many of the same challenges as black women in white male–dominated industries. Like her, I know what it means to agent myself, to go for broke to get the role I want, to fight for that seat at the table, and to be my own advocate in a room full of people who don't look like me or share my story and experiences. Working as an actor most of my life, I've learned how to speak up and refuse to accept less than what I know I deserve.

But what about you?

If you could fully center your own dreams, ideas, thoughts, and desires . . . if you were released to pursue the best version of yourself . . . if you tapped into the courage to be your biggest champion, who could you be? What goals would you accomplish? What dreams would you manifest?

In this book, Nicole reveals her incredible journey and how she got where she is today. Reading page after page, you will not only feel the same warrior energy she gives as she fights for her clients, you will also gain the knowledge you need to put in the work at the right time, in the right place, and with the right people to achieve the success you desire.

Nicole Lynn is an all-star—one of the best and brightest who knows the struggle, yet has come out on top. She wrote this book so you can come through, too, and accomplish everything you set out to do. Nothing would move her more than to help you live out your greatest potential.

Let us lift her up in the light of goodness and hold her there.

—Gabrielle Union

INTRODUCTION

You picked up this book for a reason.

Maybe you're struggling to find your purpose in life. Maybe you're trying to land your dream job. Maybe you've been clawing your way up the corporate ladder and trying to get a seat at the table. Or maybe you're trying to find just a sliver of peace to claim for yourself.

Regardless of your situation, it's time. Time for you to walk in your purpose. Time for you to claim your peace. I want you to believe this is possible, with your entire heart. No longer will you be stagnant in this life, just going through the motions. No longer will you be content with staying in your comfort zone. No longer will you have a goal that you aren't working toward.

And this adventure begins with asking yourself a question I've asked myself almost every day for the past three decades:

What do you want in life?

My answer to this question guides every big decision I make. It's the reason I worked on Wall Street, earned my law degree, and became a sports agent—think Jerry Maguire with five-inch heels and red lipstick.

In an athlete's career, aside from family, no one is more important than his or her agent.

Imagine that you have an amazing agent to help you navigate life. Someone pushing you to achieve your dreams. Someone advocating for you in rooms you haven't even walked into yet. Someone protecting the boundaries you didn't know you needed.

Now, imagine that agent is *you!*

Maybe you're like me and have an inner drive that burns bright and strong. You already work hard and are more than qualified to assume a bigger role with more responsibility and independence. But you haven't yet experienced the kinds of successes you saw for yourself. You're motivated to go after your dream, but you're not sure where to begin. Or maybe you're still searching for your life's purpose.

I'm going to let you in on a little secret. Along my life's path, I wasn't motivated to get into the business of sports because I loved football, or even because of visions like having wealth or being famous. The answer to the question of what I wanted in life was and is simple: I want to help people. In particular, I want to help people who had an upbringing like mine and are finding their own way up and out and need an advocate.

Just as I do with all my top clients, I'm here to help *you.* Because you are your own first-round pick.

To show you what I mean, here's a thought exercise: Let's pretend, for a minute, that you hire me to be your agent. I'm the person whose job it is to get you out of your cubicle and into a corner office, to finally make that big-time career pivot to more fulfilling work, or help you increase your earnings so that you can fulfill desires to travel, pay off debt, or live with financial security. What action steps would I instruct you to take? Which people should you meet with, and how should you position yourself to make major moves?

This book will show you the way forward. I'll share everything I've learned over the course of thirty years, climbing corporate ladders and finally getting a seat at the table.

I know you can be your own agent. Because I did it—and am still doing it for myself. I'm telling you, hand to God, that no matter where you come from and no matter what obstacles stand in your way, this book can help you reach your goals. I've got you.

•   •   •

Earlier, I mentioned my upbringing, and I think it's important for you to know a little about my background.

By the time I was fourteen, the house I lived in had been robbed ten times. Which was ironic, since we were poor. Dirt poor. No heat in the winter, no running water, roach-infested poor. Empty bellies poor. If we had anything to eat, it was because the elementary school sent us needy kids home with a backpack containing sandwiches and fruit cups, or my dad had a couple bucks in his pocket and thought to buy my brother Julius and me a McDonald's hamburger, which in the early nineties cost seventy-nine cents. The only thing I ever saw in the refrigerator were cans of soda. For years, I vowed never to drink the stuff.

In such a house, you'd think there'd be nothing worth stealing. But someone always seemed to notice when my dad scraped together enough money for a loaner television or a stereo from Rent-A-Center. The setup never lasted more than a few days. It quickly stopped surprising me when I'd get up in the morning and find the electronics had been stolen overnight. This was a normal part of my life, growing up in what I'd later realize was likely a trap house, located in an impoverished neighborhood of Tulsa, Oklahoma.

Even though my mother couldn't provide for our material needs, she did give me something intangible and eternal, something of value that could never be stolen: a foundation of faith in God and Jesus Christ, which provided an anchor amid the hardship and chaos.

The first time we were robbed at gunpoint, when I was eight years old, stays with me. It was summer, and I was asleep in the middle bedroom—the one without windows that had a burned-out bulb in the light fixture—when yelling woke me up. Two men were shouting at April, an acquaintance of my father who stayed in the house sometimes, to give them her jewelry.

"These were my mother's rings!" she cried out. "It's the only memory I have left of her! Please let me keep them!"

I crawled off the mattress and into a corner behind the door, hoping that anyone who looked inside the bedroom wouldn't see me. *Jesus, help me!* I silently screamed, hugging my knees to my chest, tears streaming down my face. Blood throbbed in my eyes, and I breathed as quietly as possible. *It's 1:00 a.m., so Dad should be home soon. There's no light to turn on, so they won't find me in the darkness.* I repeated these facts like mantras.

The men hollered at April and one said, "We're not going to put up with this bullsh*t," and then the voices went quiet. When the bedroom door swung open, my heart dropped. To my surprise, it was April. She didn't see me—I don't think she even realized I was inside—and she tossed the rings into the darkness, to hide them from the intruders, and closed the door behind her. The silence that followed was physically painful.

I didn't know it, but the men had left the house. They eventually returned, along with a woman, who harassed April and hit her hard enough that I heard April fall to the floor. Before I could talk myself out of it, I jumped up and ran to them.

"Don't hurt her!" I bellowed with as much force as my small body could muster. My presence shocked all four of them, and I cloaked myself in the confusion to rescue April. I reached for her hand, and just as I grasped it, I was snatched up by the neck and felt cold metal on my face. The barrel of a gun pressed against my temple.

The room thundered, and I didn't make a sound. I closed my eyes and appealed to God to forgive my sins. *This is the moment I will die, at the age of eight years old, and I hope He accepts me into heaven.*

I don't know how long we were like that, suspended in chaos, and to be honest, I can't recall how the scene ended. All I remember is that the coldness receded, April grabbed my arm, and we slipped out the back door, climbing over a fence and sprinting until our lungs gave out.

• • •

What happened that night should have broken me. And if not that night, one of the thousand other horrors I endured should have done me in. But somehow, that never happened. I don't know how to explain why not, except to say that I wouldn't let it—that was not my path.

In the absence of anyone looking out for me, I learned to look out for myself, as well as my brother. I made sure he had something to eat, and I oversaw his schoolwork. I earned straight As and was committed to extracurricular activities. When there wasn't enough money to cover all the utilities, I learned about the workarounds, like jimmying the lateral line to the water main for an hour a day, so my brother and I could take showers—cold showers, because the heat was always disconnected.

When I was in junior high, I applied to the magnet high school, filling out the paperwork and collecting the recommendations myself, and I was admitted. The high school was ranked number one in the state, and I spent hours on public buses, traveling between home, the high school, and my job at Chick-fil-A. After a few months of working, I bought a used Dodge Neon for $2,500 and a forged driver's license. That was me at age fourteen.

It's painful to look back on these years, but when I do, a few things seem clear. First, that Family & Children's Services failed us. Every day, I waited for someone to show up and save my brother and me. Our teachers all knew we lived in squalor and danger. It's a miracle we survived. And I know that I've defied what should have been my fate. My younger brother, whom I love and to whom I give lots of grace, went down a very different path, though I couldn't tell you why. For me, I always knew I wanted to accomplish great things, and I saw no reason that the circumstances of my birth should undermine my ambition. And frankly, I didn't realize until many years later that my upbringing was so different from that of my classmates. I knew we were penniless and that other families had money for new cars and cool clothes and vacations. But I didn't realize that other children weren't put through hell.

I don't think there's a straight line between my childhood and the fact that I became an agent. But what's clear as day is that my upbringing absolutely shaped the *kind* of agent I am. The people I represent—athletes, rappers, dancers—have something in common: life didn't lay out an easy road for them, and they used their talents and perseverance to succeed. For them, I'm more than a person who wheels and deals. I wear many hats: attorney, negotiator, life coach, mentor, friend, travel agent, personal assistant, therapist, cheerleader, hustler, and the list goes on. When it comes to my clients, I do it all. For instance, with my athletes, my goal is to ensure they have the best opportunities for their career, they're protecting their mental health, and they have a job that aligns with their purpose when their professional sports career ends.

• • •

This book can be read from start to finish, but you also can pick out the chapters that most apply to or resonate with you and dive into those. And be sure to complete the action items at the end of each chapter, to propel you forward. (For your convenience and quick reference, all the end-of-chapter exercises have been included in an appendix as well.) You'd better believe I give my top athletes homework too. Certain topics will take priority at different points in your life and career, so a topic that doesn't hit home now may arise in the future, and it's important to be open to shifting gears and working on those areas too.

By the time you finish this book, my hope is that you will have downloaded an inner agent into *you*. It all starts with finding your purpose. Then you can decide where you're going, and you'll have the confidence of knowing that, if you can get into the room, you will win! Together, we'll figure out what's between you and your potential. It's sure to involve plenty of discomfort, vulnerability, and hard work, but you can be certain that you've got what it takes—after all, it's what you were made for. It's time to be your own advocate, to negotiate your own deal, to take control of your own life, and to make your own rules. It's time to agent *you*.

CHAPTER ONE

Find Your Purpose

"Find your purpose or you're wasting air."
—Nipsey Hussle, "Victory Lap"

I f you've ever heard me speak live or listened to me on a podcast or attended a workshop I've taught, you've undoubtedly heard me say this phrase: "If you are not walking in your purpose, you are just working and living to die." I hope that statement shakes you to your core. I hope that statement makes your stomach sink and makes you feel uncomfortable. I hope it lights a fire in you and makes you question everything.

How we use our time while on this earth is the most important decision we'll make in our lives—and the goal should be to use this time by walking in our purpose. When you google the definition of purpose, this is what you'll read: "The reason for which something is done or created or for which something exists." Powerful words. When determining your life's purpose, you're determining the reason for which you exist, the reason for which you were created.

Wait. So, you're saying we weren't put on this earth to work really hard, gain and lose ten pounds over and over again, get in debt, then get out of debt, go on a fancy vacation, and then die?

Of course we weren't.

We are each placed on this earth for a specific reason. This chapter is going to help you identify that reason. And listen, I get it. Every blog, every podcast, every influencer is talking about "living in your purpose." It's the new fad. Although I recognize it's a trend, I'd be remiss not to talk about it in this book, because I believe nothing is more important than walking in your purpose.

Sometimes we overcomplicate the conversation about finding purpose. We assume that finding purpose involves an intricate, difficult task, like curing AIDS or ending world hunger. However, finding purpose is as simple as determining that the thing you're doing every day is the thing you're meant to be doing.

When you start the journey to identify your purpose, it may feel like you're on a road trip without a map. You take one highway and discover you're on the wrong highway, so you quickly exit and end up on the feeder road. You try to get back on the highway, but each of the entrances is blocked. So, you take a detour. The next thing you know, you're back on the highway, going the wrong way. Then you're on a side street. Then you're in a dead-end cul-de-sac and don't know how to exit. The journey to find purpose can take you on many different routes. I'm sure some of you reading this book right now have changed professions even two or three times. Started and ended businesses. Had passions that died off and then found new ones.

It annoys the crap out of me when authors and speakers talk about purpose while also seemingly hiding the ball. Like: "Oh, I'm so happy I'm walking in my purpose! What a blessing and an honor blah blah blah" (eye roll). *Thanks, lady, but give me the secret recipe!* These people make finding your purpose sound difficult, like it's reserved for an elite group.

News flash, people: Everyone has a purpose, and finding your purpose should not be hard. Period. In fact, your purpose was placed deep inside of you when you were born, and now it's just a matter of bringing that part of you to light, of discovering more of who you are. More of what makes you . . . you.

As someone who believes I am absolutely walking in my purpose, I want to help you do the same. Therefore, I've simplified how to determine what your purpose is and boiled down purpose to four criteria. I believe your life's purpose is:

1. Something you're naturally good at;
2. Something you enjoy;
3. Something that makes an impact in the world; and
4. Something you would do for free.

If you can check off all four of these items, you're likely already living in your purpose. And I know there's someone out there right now saying: "This is dumb. I'm in my purpose for sure, but I can only mark off three out of those four items." While it's not a perfect formula, I do think it will help point you in the right direction.

Let's break down each of these criteria.

SOMETHING YOU ARE NATURALLY GOOD AT: YOUR SUPERPOWER

I sat on a panel with Microsoft vice president Lani Phillips. When asked about what she thought purpose was, she defined it as someone's superpower—the thing that comes naturally to you. And I couldn't agree more.

For instance, when you think about Superman, you probably think of his ability to fly. When you think about the Hulk, you probably think of his superhuman strength. What do people think about when they think of you? What is your "superpower"?

I don't want you to make this difficult. Instead, think of the thing your friends identify as your strength. They might say things like, "Oh, Nicole is really good at that," or "We could ask Taylor—she's got a knack for that." It doesn't even have to be something you were taught or went to school for. Take a second and make a list of these things; maybe you have four or five things you excel at. That list will narrow as we apply additional factors.

If you're having trouble with this list, ask some of your trusted family or friends. This might be uncomfortable, but their perspectives can be valuable for this exercise. You might be surprised at some of the things that you overlook, because, well, they come naturally to you! That's a good thing— that's your superpower.

SOMETHING YOU ENJOY

———————

Your purpose should be something you enjoy. I don't believe we were put on this earth for a purpose that makes us miserable. So, ask yourself: Of the items on this list, what do I enjoy? What can I lose track of time while doing it? Maybe it's dancing, and your purpose is to reach people through your performances. Can you dance for what seems like just a few minutes, and the next thing you know, two or three hours have passed? Or maybe you're on a church committee, and you enjoy serving each Sunday in any capacity: greeting people, taking up offerings, or praying at the end. Maybe you've always been good at art, and when it comes to designing clothes, you could sit for hours on end drawing your dream pieces.

Now, I won't say you have to enjoy your purpose all the time, because the journey to get to living in your purpose could be filled with obstacles. And just because it's your purpose doesn't mean it comes without grueling, hard work. My life as a sports agent is a living testament to that (keep reading—we'll get to that later in the book). But I do believe that when you finally reach the destination, you will enjoy it. Walking in your purpose should bring you fulfillment and joy, but that doesn't always equate to happiness along the way. Even after a really tough day—possibly with tears involved—you should be able to look back and say, "This is what I was meant to do." So, take a look at your list and cross off any items you happen to be good at but wouldn't enjoy doing.

SOMETHING THAT MAKES AN IMPACT ON THE WORLD

Your purpose should have an impact on the world. Again, don't make this complicated. Some of the obvious ways to make an impact include fighting for social justice, donating funds to a charity you care about, curing a disease, starting a nonprofit for homeless kids, and so forth. But here are a few other ways you may not have considered:

- Being a mom or dad and raising kids to be good humans
- Adopting a dog from a homeless shelter
- Creating jewelry that makes the owner smile
- Making people laugh through your comedy
- Taking things off someone's plate by being an executive assistant
- Coaching softball for middle school girls and teaching them the value of teamwork
- Being a loving husband or wife to a spouse who needs love

All of these, plus many more, impact the world and shouldn't be overlooked. Don't let the world or society tell you what an impact is or isn't. You define this on your own terms, as everyone is impacted differently.

In case no one has told you: your purpose and your impact don't have to be your day job. Let me say that again in a different way: what you do to pay the bills doesn't have to be your life's purpose. I'm a civil litigation attorney who represents some of the world's biggest companies. I handle high-level, complex, commercial litigation cases like breach of contract claims. Would I say I'm making an impact on the world by saving these Fortune 500 companies money and protecting them from liability? If I'm being honest, and by my definition of impact, I'd have to say no, I feel I'm making zero personal impact. Yes, I am good at being an attorney and I enjoy it, but I don't feel I'm making an impact on the world through this work. Thus, I don't find purpose in my day job. My purpose lies outside of that.

Maybe you'll find purpose in your side hustle or your hobby or in your personal life or in your friendships or in your marriage. And, hey, maybe you're one of the lucky ones whose purpose is in your work, and every single day you get paid for your calling. Either way, it's important that whatever you deem your purpose is, it's something that makes a lasting impact.

Look at your list again. You've narrowed down the things you are good at and crossed off the ones you wouldn't enjoy. Now, remove those you don't deem impactful. Perhaps this list only has a couple items left, and you're that much closer to determining your purpose.

It's now time to apply the "purpose test" to the remaining items on your list.

THE PURPOSE TEST:
WOULD YOU DO IT FOR FREE?

As long as I can remember, I've always known exactly what I wanted to do in life. I may not have always known it was called a *sports agent,* but I knew I wanted to help athletes. I never wavered on this, and every career step I took was to reach this goal.

I still recall the day I finally received the confirmation I needed to know I was truly walking in my purpose. It was a few years ago, and I was in my second year as an NFL agent. I was walking around my neighborhood with my best friend, telling her how excited I was to have successfully negotiated my first contract for a client. To me, a junior agent, the contract had taken forever. So much back-and-forth, so many days of research, and true negotiation skills. I was so relieved it was done, and I also was proud of myself for this accomplishment.

As I told her the story, she said: "That's really great! So, how much money do you think you'll take home from that deal when your commission comes out?"

I stopped in my tracks. "Commission?" I asked. Not one time while in law school, while studying for the NFL agent exam, while applying to sports agencies, or even while recruiting this particular player did I ever think about what I'd be paid.

I looked at her with a blank stare and said, "Wow, oh my gosh—I forgot that I get *paid* to do this." And that was the moment. Right there, standing in the middle of my neighborhood, sweating like a pig (because of the hundred-degree Texas heat), I knew I was truly walking in my purpose! The entire time I had negotiated this player's contract, it never crossed my mind that this was a job I was doing, and I'd be compensated for my work. So, when I realized I'd be making money—cash money—off of the deal I'd worked so hard on, this was an added bonus. The money clearly didn't faze me, and it had nothing to do with *why* I was in this profession. I was in this profession because it's my purpose.

I call this the "purpose test." I was doing something I was good at, something I enjoyed, and something that was making an impact every single day with young athletes. Even so, it wasn't until I acknowledged I'd do this job for *free* that I knew it was truly something I was called to do. When you're struggling to determine if you're truly walking in your purpose, ask yourself: If you didn't need money, would you do this activity for free? For example, do you love blogging so much that you'd do it forever and not worry about what it brought in? Does the idea of owning your own business and being an entrepreneur excite you, or the funds that come from that job? The answer to the purpose test is how you'll know.

Let me be abundantly clear about something: I do want to make money, and lots of it. Just because you want to make money doesn't mean that gig isn't your purpose. The purpose test simply asks about the initial excitement. Is the initial excitement about owning your own business and working for yourself, and the money is secondary? Is the initial excitement that you get to star in movies and walk on the red carpet and then, as an afterthought, you get paid too?

In that moment while walking around my neighborhood, I not only wanted to make money, I also *needed* to make money. I was drowning in law school debt and supporting my extended family back home. I had no help, so the money was necessary. But the money was my secondary excitement. Representing some of the biggest names in football was the primary excitement.

Even in writing this book, I didn't think about how much I could earn from writing it. I'm writing this book because I genuinely like helping people reach their full potential—it is part of my calling and my purpose. If I make money off the book, that's an added bonus (and would be nice), but the money isn't my motivation. In applying the purpose test to writing this book, the money is secondary; thus, it passes the test.

Take some time to decide if what you're doing passes the purpose test. Ask yourself: What is the initial excitement? Is it the act? Or is it the money?

I hope you now have something remaining on your list that you're naturally good at, that you enjoy, that makes an impact on the world, and, if you had to, that you would do for free.

WHY DOES PURPOSE MATTER?

Imagine some of our greatest heroes throughout history and throughout the world. Imagine if they'd never found their life's purpose. When I think about people who realized and spent time determining their purpose, Nelson Mandela always comes to mind. How different might the world look if he hadn't walked in his calling? Because he put in that time and effort, the world is able to reap the benefits of his dedication. Many people throughout history have made a lasting impact on the world by simply doing what they were called to do. And even if these individuals aren't household names—for instance, those who've invented vaccines and lifesaving technologies—their passion has impacted and will continue to impact the world for generations to come.

Whether or not you're religious, the biblical story of Esther is, in many ways, ultimately about purpose. At the beginning of the story, we find a young Jewish orphan named Esther. Esther and her people had been taken captive in a foreign land for many years. However, even as an orphaned captive, through a series of events, she's elevated to the position of queen.

Based on the beginning of the story, one might think her life's purpose was to become queen. But her actual life's purpose was rescuing her people, the Jews. As queen, Esther becomes instrumental, if not essential, in rescuing her people from torture and mass annihilation.

My favorite line in this story is in Esther 4:14. As Esther was preparing to use her "superpower" as queen to request that the king save her people, she was told these critical words: "And who knows but that you have come to your royal position for such a time as this?"

Maybe *you* were called for such a time as this. Maybe *you* were put on this earth to counsel that woman walking through depression. To help that young man learn about finances and get out of debt. To paint that masterpiece that will hang on the living room wall of a newly married couple, making their house a home. Who knows? There is someone out there right now waiting on you to realize your purpose.

It's time to realize your calling. When you walk in your purpose, you'll have a sense of self-worth like you've never known before. Make finding your purpose the most important mission in your life. The world needs what only you can offer.

AGENT YOU:
TAKE ACTION!

1. Use the steps provided in this chapter to identify your purpose. Make a list of four or five things you're really good at, then cross off any item that doesn't meet the following criteria:

   * Things you truly enjoy;
   * Things that impact the world; and
   * Things you would do for free, if money were no object.

   After this process, you should only have one, perhaps two items on your list.

2. Find a way to walk in your purpose. If you're already living out your purpose, congratulations! However, if you aren't, you may need to find the time and energy to make this a reality. Think of at least one or two ways, small or large, that enable you to start walking in your purpose today.

3. Begin planning for the long term. Even if you have other commitments keeping you from walking fully in your purpose right now, it's never too late to start planning for the future. In a journal, a note on your phone, or a document on your computer, start envisioning how your day-to-day life will look when you're walking in your purpose. Think about

not only the practical elements, but the positive mental and emotional benefits that walking in your purpose will have on you.

Everyone has
a purpose—
including you!

CHAPTER TWO

Get Your Dream Job

We've talked about finding your purpose, and maybe now you're excited, thinking, *Okay, I have the dream. Now, how do I get the job?*

The number one question I get asked is how I landed my dream job. How did you break into the business? How did you get your first shot? How do I do it too?

I get it. Every time I watch one of my clients play in his first NFL game, I get chills thinking, *Wow. I get to do this!* So, I understand why I get asked the question often. I feel blessed to work in a field that is truly a dream come true, and I want everyone to be able to look at their careers and say, "Wow. I get to do this!" No matter if your dream job is to be a sports agent or a model or a singer or a publisher or an inventor or whatever, I've written this chapter with specific tips just for you.

MAKE "SOMEDAY" TODAY
(SMALL THINGS FOR BIG RESULTS)

Not knowing your purpose is scary, but knowing your purpose and not walking in it is scarier. Here's how I can usually determine whether people know their purpose or calling but aren't walking in it: they use the word *someday*.

"Someday, I'm going to start my own business."

"Someday, I'm going to ask her on a date."

"Someday, I'm going to quit my job and chase my dream job."

Someday, someday, someday!

Let me tell you something I hope wakes you up right now: you can *someday* yourself out of a life. Someday, you'll wake up and ten years have passed, and all you've done is dream and waste time. Someday may never come. Someday, you're dead.

Yes, that might sound extreme, but this is an extremely common phenomenon. The term *midlife crisis* exists for a reason.

How do you get a dream job? You make someday today. Hearing that probably puts you on edge. You may be thinking, *I can't just quit my job today. I can't just make the move today. I can't just start the business today . . . I can't!*

Don't worry—I'm not asking you to take all the necessary steps today. But let me tell you what you *can* do. You can do *something* toward your dream today, versus someday. You can take one step forward. Can you scope out potential locations for the boutique you plan to open someday? Can you buy the books needed to start preparing for medical school, which you plan to attend someday?

You can always do something today toward your goals. Take the small steps today, so you can someday walk in your purpose and someday have your dream job.

I want to take a second to remind you that this book isn't meant to be a casual read. This book is designed to help you take action. I want you to walk away from reading this book with a plan, with lists, with ideas, and, God willing, with *purpose*.

So, here is your action: Make a list of five small things you can do each day toward your goal or dream job. Each day, reference this list and pick something to do that day toward your goal. If you have to, schedule this activity in your calendar, so you can't ignore it. The hope is that you'll do something off of this list almost every day. It's important to include some super-easy things on your list, for the days you don't feel like doing much, if anything. For example, on a day you aren't feeling it, you could just "brainstorm." You can do that in the shower for five minutes. Listing some easier tasks will help you with consistency. Completing these tasks, no matter how small, will also keep you motivated. Who doesn't get satisfaction from crossing something off your to-do list? Just me?

After you complete your list, start a new one. This way, you are always, always working toward getting to your dream and doing it today instead of someday. If you hope to start your own business, here are examples of five small things you could have on your list:

1. Pick out a name.
2. Register your LLC with the secretary of state.

3. Research the market.
4. Look up potential products you plan to sell and find a wholesaler.
5. Create a logo.

Here are examples of five small things you can have on the list if your target is to relocate for your dream job:

1. Start a separate savings account for the move.
2. Find a real estate agent who will notify you when a house or apartment in your budget becomes available.
3. Look up the requirements to switch out your license and car title.
4. Start downsizing to make the move easier; sell anything you don't absolutely love.
5. Find a church or community group to join when you move, so you will have a tribe.

None of these five things are the actual move, because the move will come at some point in the future. But these tasks are at least setting you up for when someday comes.

Put this book down right now and make your list of five small things. The easiest place to save this list is in a journal or in the notes app on your phone. You'll need it to be easily accessible, because you'll hopefully reference it daily. I also want you to title this list "Someday." That way, every time you look at this list, you're reminded that someday is *today*!

SHOOT YOUR PROFESSIONAL SHOT

When I decided I wanted to be a sports agent, I reached out to more than a hundred people in sports to try to break into the business. I wasn't afraid to shoot my professional shot. Let's talk about how to effectively shoot your professional shot, so you don't miss it.

When you reach out to someone asking for help or insight into an industry, be specific with your questions. Questions such as "Can you mentor me?" or "Can you tell me how you got into the business?" are unlikely to be answered. Think about it: Why would someone mentor you if they don't know you? It can be perceived as a presumptuous ask. And questions about how someone got into the business usually have complex answers. Even thinking of my own story, I couldn't type the entire response into one email if I wanted to. That question can be overwhelming. This is why I always recommend asking specific questions: "Do you recommend I take XYZ course to reach my goal?" or "How many hours a week did you put into your side hustle before reaching success?" I'm more inclined to answer specific questions and ignore those that will take more time to answer.

Another tip to shooting your professional shot is to respect people's time by offering to treat them to coffee. I can't tell you how many times someone who wants to get into sports asks to take me to lunch or dinner to pick my brain. Lunch and dinner are a commitment. A meal is at least two hours long and, honestly, it can be awkward with someone you don't know. Coffee is always easier.

When asking someone to coffee, let them know the time commitment: "Hi, Mary. I'd love to buy you coffee and pick your brain for ten to fifteen minutes." Giving away thirty minutes may sound like nothing to you, but for someone who is asked this several times a week, that time adds up. Thus, ten to fifteen minutes is an easier ask and more considerate of the person's time.

Usually, when someone asks for fifteen minutes, I end up giving them more time, but there is peace in knowing I'm not forced to talk for a longer period than I can fit in my schedule. Booking a shorter session gives the individual the opportunity to choose how long to spend with you. Also, once you're at the coffee, keep track of the time. When you hit the fifteen-minute mark, let the person know and offer to end the session. Like I said, more often than not, you may be able to squeeze in some extra time. But, more important, you've signaled that you are professional, honest, and respectful.

Another way to shoot your professional shot is to find creative ways to get in front of the people with whom you hope to talk. I remember several occasions when I was speaking at an event, and afterward, someone would come up to me and say something like, "I drove four hours just to hear you speak and get the opportunity to meet you." Listen, I'm not recommending you guilt-trip people, but if someone went to great lengths to meet me, I feel obligated to give them some of my time. I respect their dedication.

To that same point, find ways to get in front of people that don't require them to do anything. For example, if you want to meet me and you know I'll be at a certain football game, you might offer to meet me at the concession stand for five minutes. Some of you may be reading this and thinking: *How insane is that? I'd never fly to a football game just to meet someone for five minutes.* Well, that's because your dream most likely doesn't involve being in sports. But let's say your dream is to be signed to a large record label, and you know the vice president of Atlantic Records is going to be at a brunch in your city. If you were serious about this dream job, you'd be at that brunch, résumé in hand.

My last tip for shooting your professional shot is to *give a little.* What can you offer the person you're reaching out to? Of course, we all hope that people will take our call out of the goodness of their hearts (because, duh, we live in a perfect world with perfect people, right?). But that won't always be the case.

When I broke into the sports world, I reached out to a lot of sports agents, but none returned my call. One agent, Ken Sarnoff, represented many of my college friends. So, in emailing him, I used that as leverage, letting him know that some of his biggest clients were people I was close to. Lucky for me, that got him to respond.

In a phone conversation, he explained to me how horrible the business is and made a genuine effort to dissuade me from being a sports agent (I don't blame him for his sentiments, as I now share many of the same thoughts), and he gave me some great advice. He said, "Look, I get this call four times a week and, no offense to you, but why would I be inclined to help you, out of all the new, young agents out there who message me?" He added: "If you could, say, get me a meeting with one of the top players in college football, sure, maybe I would hear you out. But you have to bring something to the table to show you are serious about this industry."

At the time, one of the biggest names in college football was an offensive lineman at a Division I school in Texas. I hung up, and about twenty minutes later, I called Ken back.

"Hello," he said, in a sort of thrown-off voice. "Did you need something else?"

"No," I responded. "But the player wants to know if you can talk tomorrow at 4:00 p.m."

Ken was shocked, but in that exact moment, he realized I added value, and the rest is history.

What can you bring to the table? What is your value add that the person who has access to your dream job would find intriguing or helpful?

Shooting your professional shot for a dream opportunity requires you to think outside the box. It requires you to do things others wouldn't even think of. You may have heard the famous quote by Jerry Rice, an NFL Hall of Fame wide receiver who played for the San Francisco 49ers: "Today I will do what others won't! So tomorrow I can accomplish what others can't."[1] Repeat it. Internalize it. Let this be your life's mantra as you chase your dream job.

WORK FOR EXPERIENCE

To land your dream job, you must be willing to do whatever it takes. Let's explore this more and talk about working for experience. When people ask for advice on how to get their dream job, I have a lot to say (heck, I wrote an entire book about it). But in my mind, one piece of advice always stands above the rest: Be willing to work for experience. Many times

I see a person's desire to walk in his or her purpose collide and crash with their desire to be rich. You *can* walk in your purpose and become wealthy, *but both do not always happen at the same time.*

Before I explain further, I want to be clear that I believe all people should be paid their worth. I am an advocate for equal pay and being paid what you deserve! But when you're chasing a dream opportunity that only comes around once in a lifetime, you have to find a way to set yourself apart, and sometimes that means working just for the experience.

And look, I get it. Because of your financial situation, sometimes working for free isn't an option. You have to make decisions that will protect you and your family. (Thankfully, many companies are also recognizing that some young adults aren't in a position to work for free, so paid internships are becoming more common.) However, if you can work solely to gain experience, or at an extremely discounted rate, I urge you to consider it. Get creative. Maybe you don't work completely for free, but you can feasibly do certain aspects of the work without pay. Maybe this will have to be your side hustle for a while, as you gain momentum. While you might not be exchanging your services for cash, in the long term, garnering exposure, building your portfolio, and gaining experience can sometimes be more valuable than money.

Surprisingly, experience itself can be hard to gain. By working for free, you're setting yourself up to gain that valuable experience. For example, if you want to be a famous celebrity makeup artist but have never done a celebrity's makeup, when a celebrity comes to your town, consider offering your services for free the first time. The experience you'll get while providing this service is worth way more than money. Now you've done a celebrity's makeup, and the celebrity is aware of who you are. The next time she's in town, she's more likely to call you first because she knows you're good at what you do, and she'll be willing to pay you for those services (win!). You also have a celebrity name to add to your client roster, which helps legitimatize you to future celebrity clientele.

When I decided to become a media agent and represent on-air talent, I knew that my biggest challenge was my lack of experience in this area. Yes, I was an attorney, and yes, I had represented talent before, but not this specific type. So, when I signed my first on-air talent as a media agent, I offered to do her broadcasting deal with ESPN for free. That way, I got the needed experience, I set myself apart from veteran media agents, and I had less pressure to be perfect, because I wasn't charging. I took this same approach when I negotiated my first record deal for a rapper: I did it for free.

What services can you offer someone for free that could help you get the exposure or experience you need? If your dream job is to be a model, and a local business needs a model to wear their clothes in photographs, do it for free. The shoot will give you more experience and practice modeling, and the posted pictures will help you gain exposure. If your dream is to be a publicist for athletes, offer to do their first public relations placement for free, so you can demonstrate your skills. If your dream job is to work for a politician, ask if you can volunteer for their campaign. It will give you the behind-the-scenes experience and up-close-and-personal exposure with the politician.

Just know this: when you're walking in your purpose, the money will come eventually. But while chasing your dream job, don't let your desire to make money hinder you from getting both experience and exposure. One day, you'll charge whatever you want and won't waver on your prices. But be patient—there are levels to this.

THE JUMP

In 1984, the Boston College Eagles trailed the defending national champions, the Miami Hurricanes, by four points. In a last-ditch attempt to score, Eagles quarterback Doug Flutie threw what would become the most famous Hail Mary of all time, allowing the Eagles to upset the Miami Hurricanes by three points. In football, a Hail Mary is a long forward pass made in desperation, usually toward the end zone, with only a small chance of success. Even though the likelihood of scoring is slim, a Hail Mary has the ability to change the outcome of a game unlike any other play.

A Hail Mary is no different in the real world. Ask successful people their story, and I promise you that each of them can tell you about their "Hail Mary": The pivotal moment that single-handedly changed the trajectory of their life or career. The one big moment that had to happen in order for them to get where they are now, and usually a moment that wasn't easy. For Mark Zuckerberg, it was dropping out of Harvard and starting Facebook; for Bill Gates, it was investing money into Microsoft; for Jeff Bezos, it was quitting his high-paying investment banking job at the age of thirty to start an online bookselling website out of his garage—which we now know as Amazon.com.[2] The real-life Hail Mary is the gut-wrenching move you have to take that makes you sick to your stomach to think about, but that you know has to be done to reach your goal.

I want you to take a moment and contemplate what exactly is holding you back from your dream job or from your ultimate goal. What is your Hail Mary? I challenge you to sit down right now and list every single thing holding you back from your goal. Go—write them down! What's the biggest contributor on the list? Usually, the biggest obstacle to you taking the next step is your "Hail Mary."

My Hail Mary was when I walked into my boss's office and quit my position at a top-ranked investment banking firm. I remember like it was yesterday. I had moved to New York City the year before to start a job I received only by the favor of God. A "dream job" for many, but a stepping stone for me. I'd stayed up all night, preparing what I'd say to my boss. And even when writing it, I couldn't help asking myself, *Am I losing my mind? Am I making a mistake?*

When I walked into my boss's office the next morning, I was holding back tears. Not because I'd miss the work, but because I knew that if this decision didn't pan out, I had no plan B. I had no family to fall back on, I had no trust fund, I had nothing. If this decision didn't turn out as I expected, I'd have to answer only to myself for it.

I walked into her office and realized there was no turning back. "I'm going to law school," I said. "I drafted this entire professional statement to tell you, but I am weirdly drawing a blank, so I'll tell you the truth. I want to feel fulfilled in whatever I do, and I do not feel it here. I am going to chase a dream of mine, and I hope one day you'll hear about this very successful sports agent and you'll say, 'Wow, she used to work here.' And I hope when that day comes, your final thought will be, *I am so glad she quit.*"

I left a prestigious financial analyst position on Wall Street to pursue a dream of sports, while everybody was calling me crazy. In what world does a person who grew up homeless leave a cushy, six-figure job on a hunch? *That* is a Hail Mary. I would not be where I am today had I not taken that risk, had I not thrown that Hail Mary. If it doesn't already, I'm certain that your story, your journey, your dream, includes a Hail Mary. You just have to figure out what it is.

THE TIME TO FAIL IS NOW

Here's a big obstacle I've seen with people following through with their dreams: they expect to be an immediate success. We see the "overnight successes" and romanticize the idea of becoming an instant hit. We've done the purpose test, and we've identified the dream job. So, why wouldn't we automatically land that celebrity client or develop the next *Shark Tank* invention? However, that is not reality. When I left Wall Street at age twenty-three to chase what may have seemed like a pipe dream, I wasn't immediately successful. As a matter of fact, I was far from it. (Don't worry—we'll get to my not-so-pretty moments later in the book.) When I decided to make the leap into sports, I knew how difficult it would be to get a job, and I knew I could fail. But most important, I knew that if I wanted to succeed, I needed to fail early.

I cannot say this enough: the time to fail is now. Maybe I'm speaking to you, a twenty- or thirtysomething, unmarried (or newly married), no kids, searching for purpose. There is no better time to fail than the present, and your circumstances prove that. You're at the beginning of your career, not the pinnacle, and you have yet to build an empire, so the likelihood of anything crashing and burning is slim. (What do you have to crash and burn anyway?) The earlier you fail, the more time you have to rebuild anything that is lost along the way. It's a lot easier to start a new career now versus ten years from now. It's a lot easier to rebuild a savings account now versus when you're close to retirement. It's a lot easier to learn a new skill set, start at a new company, or switch industries right now rather than later. If you can prevent additional hardship by failing early, then do it.

With this in mind, if you're trying to determine when to throw your Hail Mary, I encourage you to think long and hard about whether there's any specific advantage to waiting. If there isn't, taking the jump now may make the most sense. Here is the hard truth: I say the time to fail is now not because I think there's a possibility of you failing, but because you *will* fail in some way, somehow. Even if it's not a massive failure, such as losing your house because you chased a dream, your journey to your dream job will come with mistakes. No one's journey is perfect.

You may be reading this and thinking: *Well, lady, I'm forty-two. Are you saying it's too late for me to start something new and fail?* Absolutely not. Yes, I believe there's convenience in being able to fail early, but not every individual has that luxury. Some people have to wait to chase their dreams. Maybe you didn't have the resources, maybe you raised a family and now it's finally your turn. Whatever your story, whatever your circumstance, it's not too late for you.

Did you know Vera Wang didn't design her first dress until the age of forty? Forty! Did you hear that? One of the world's biggest fashion designers, a former ice skater and dancer turned magazine editor, changed her mind about life at the age of forty and chased her dream job.[3] Vera Wang's story reminds us that it's never too late to go after exactly what you want. You're not too old, and you're not too late. It doesn't matter if the party has already started, as long as you get to the party eventually. I believe they call it being fashionably late.

If that doesn't motivate you, consider this: the time to fail is now, because now is all that's guaranteed. We all have only this one life to live, and many people who are no longer with us would love the chance to live and fail. So, I say this with all the authority I can: Take the jump, start the business, write the book, ask for his number, buy the shoes, quit your job, start the blog, change your career, marry her, have the baby, chase the dream job, all while you can. While you're still here. While you're still breathing. While you can still fail. The clock is ticking.

AGENT YOU: TAKE ACTION!

1. Make a list of five small things you can do to work toward your dream job.

   - If you need to schedule time each day to hold yourself accountable for completing these tasks, do so. Also, remember to include easy tasks on your list, for the days you have less time or motivation.

- When you complete this first list, start a new one—keep the momentum going.

2. Think of at least five people you can ask for a ten- to fifteen-minute commitment to have a phone conversation or grab coffee. After you do this, brainstorm ideas around the answers to the following questions:

   - How can you get in front of these people? Do you share any mutual connections? Can you direct message (DM) them on social media? Are they attending an event you can gain entrance to?
   - How can you demonstrate added value to each person on your list? Can you make a connection for them? Do you have a skill that these people or their organization are lacking?

3. Though it's not possible for everyone, consider working for experience.

   - How many hours a week could you commit to this undertaking? Setting limits from the onset will help keep you from being taken advantage of.
   - Document everything you gain from this experience: build a portfolio, list your accomplishments on your résumé, and so forth.

- If you absolutely can't work solely to gain experience, consider bartering your services. Is there someone who needs a service you can offer who also can provide you with a service?

Today is the day to start working toward your dream job.

CHAPTER THREE

Be Your Authentic Self

still remember my first NFL Scouting Combine, which wasn't that long ago. My biggest question about the week was what I would wear. I couldn't decide if I wanted to wear a ball cap, jeans, and tennis shoes, or if I wanted to wear what I'd normally wear to a conference: jeans, a blazer, heels, wavy beachy curls, and my favorite nude lipstick. I reached out to a couple agents I knew, male and female, and heard the same advice: just try to blend in. Years later, I still feel this was some of the worst advice I've ever gotten as an agent. I decided to ignore it, because it didn't sit right with me. So I put on my five-inch heels and lipstick and walked into the NFL Combine like I owned the place.

I imagine you might be thinking: *Who cares what you wear? What's the big deal?* Although it may seem like a small decision, it was career defining. Why? Because that was the day I decided I would be my 100 percent authentic self in my career as a sports agent. So, it wasn't just about heels or no heels. It was a question: Am I going to be Nicole Lynn, or am I going to be someone else? Putting on those heels was me deciding I was bringing my true self to the table. That I didn't want to blend in, because I was made to stand out.

Of course, when I walked into the room, I definitely stood out. I was okay with that, though I was still uncomfortable and nervous. However, I imagine I would've been ten times more uncomfortable if I'd walked in there as someone else. When I decided to be true to myself, that didn't stop with my attire—I was true to me in all aspects. If you follow my social media, you have probably seen a number of interesting posts, including choreographed TikTok dances with clients, secret handshakes, and me going completely nuts when one of my guys catches an interception during Monday Night Football. I call myself the "crazy agent," because you never know what you're going to get. The only thing I can promise is that you'll get the real me: the good, the bad, the ugly.

Winning on your own terms means showing up every day as *you*. Remember that your gifts, your personality, and your talents were specifically given to you by God. I genuinely believe I've made it to where I am in my career as a sports agent, and fast, because I decided to be my authentic self. Shoot, you probably wouldn't be reading this book had I not made the decision to be me. I can't imagine how different my career would look had I decided not to wear heels that day and instead opted to blend in. Again, it wasn't about the heels. It was about me making the decision that I was comfortable with showcasing myself to the world.

What does being your authentic self look like?

- *Create your own lane in industries, situations, and places that weren't necessarily designed with you in mind.* Set yourself apart by leaving the beaten path and blazing your own trail. When you're in situations where you don't fit in, don't force it. Remain true to you and create a space made perfectly for you.
- *Be okay with taking up space.* Your thoughts, your ideas, and your insight all matter, and they're *good.* You weren't meant to just live on this earth, but to take up space. Taking up space means being included and being able to provide your perspective. It means being counted in.
- *Don't be intimidated by situations and people that seem "too big."* Take pride in the value you can add to the world, and never be afraid to showcase it. Don't let anyone's status, wealth, or education intimidate you. Remember: God will qualify the called.
- *Make decisions for your life based on what you want, not what others want.* Living someone else's life or pursuing someone else's dream is exhausting. Live your life to the fullest by making decisions that align with what benefits you and makes you happy.
- *Understand that not everyone will like you.* When I realized I am not for everyone, my life changed drastically. Say it with me: "I am not for everyone." Who doesn't like you is, frankly, none of your business, so don't even try to find out. I'll let you in on a secret: It doesn't matter how good a person

you are, how genuine you are, or how much integrity you have—there will always be someone who chooses to misunderstand you. Let go of worrying about the haters or social media bullies in your comments and live your life.

Decide today that you are going to show up every day as *you*!

WHO ARE YOU?

Right now, if someone were to ask you, "Who are you?" what would you say? Take a second to answer out loud. Start with "I, (insert name), am _____." Was it easy for you to answer this question? If not, you have some work to do, because you can't be your authentic self if you don't know who you are.

I like to break down who I am into five categories:

- identity
- belief
- stance
- enjoyment
- legacy

In greater detail, these categories answer the following questions:

- What do you identify as?
- What do you believe in?
- What do you stand for and against?

- What do you enjoy?
- What do you want your legacy to be?

Here is my response to the question "Who are you?":

I, Nicole Lynn, am a black woman who believes in giving and Jesus. I stand for criminal justice reform, and I am against bullying and racism. Assisting impoverished families and being a good wife are important to me. I enjoy sports and writing. When I'm gone, I hope to be remembered as someone who loved people more than herself, someone who was compassionate and empathetic to those in need, and someone who inspired future generations to live a life full of purpose.

The above paragraph is what I call my "me statement." Everyone should have one. By reading my "me statement," you get a high-level view of who I am. Who you are is crucial to living a life of purpose and being your authentic self. You cannot find purpose and passion when you don't know who you are, what you stand for, and what you hope to leave behind. Without thinking, someone should be able to say, "I don't know Scott well, but I do know he's very serious about his family," or "I don't think that is an activity Jan would participate in, since she's passionate about gun control." If the people closest to you cannot articulate the things you stand for, the things that are important to you—Houston, we have a big problem.

Let's break down your "me statement" step-by-step.

What do you identify as? Determining your identity is the single most important prong in your "me statement." An identity includes a person's beliefs, qualities, core values, and personality, as well as external characteristics, such as gender and race. The way you're viewed also can play a role in your identity, but most important is the way you view yourself. You may view yourself as a mom, a wife, an accountant, or a comedian—thus, that's where your identity is found.

It's crucial to note that identity is a *choice.* Unfortunately, many times an identity can be forced upon us. We may internalize the identity of our parents or acquire the identity of the people we grew up around. Or our identity may be molded by our peers.

When figuring out who you are, you should spend time determining your sense of self and how that has formed over time. You also should ensure that you're being true to who you are by not adopting an identity that society has forced on you. When your identity is chosen for you, a sense of emptiness often comes with it. Doubts about self-worth, self-esteem, and purpose are all common for people who are living in an identity they didn't choose. If you only take one thing from this section, let it be this: there is so much power in finding your true self and even more power in showcasing that self to the world. Visualize how you see yourself, and then visualize how the world sees you. Do these images align? If not, consider whether you're hiding your authentic self. Let's take off the mask and live a life of choice—let's be exactly who we want to be.

What do you believe in? I believe in Jesus, in giving, in being debt free, and in Beyoncé's ability to continue to be the best performer of all time. (Hey, who doesn't believe in Beyoncé?) What you believe in helps construct your core values, the fundamental beliefs of a person or organization. These guiding principles dictate behavior and can help with decision making. Core values are typically instilled in us from a young age and can be passed down from generation to generation.

Because I believe in Jesus, many of my core values are biblical, and those values play a huge role in who I am. Because I believe in financial freedom, my core values consist of saving money and having a cushion in my budget. Because I believe that we're not meant to hoard our possessions, but instead give them to those who need them most, a core value I have is giving. Do you believe in showing respect to others? Are you someone who does everything with integrity? Take some time to determine what you believe in, and your core values will follow.

What do you stand for and against? I tend to find that it's easy to determine what people stand against (e.g., Susie is against sex trafficking, Bob is against abortion, etc.). But, for whatever reason, it's less easy to determine what people stand for! You should stand for something with so much passion and enthusiasm that people immediately associate that cause with you. The people closest to you should be able to easily identify what causes you care for deeply and things you don't tolerate.

In my "me statement," I mentioned that I stand for criminal justice reform. Because this is something I stand for, it is something I'm willing to give my time and money to. When trying to determine what someone stands for, I tend to ask people one question: What would you march in the streets for? I can assure you that no matter how much I care about gun control and immigration issues, it's unlikely that I'd march in the streets for those issues. It doesn't mean I don't find them important, because I do, but I'm allowing others to carry the burden for those issues. I stay in my lane and dedicate my resources to causes I have chosen to home in on (e.g., criminal justice reform).

We were created to have empathy about bad situations, but we weren't created to fix them all. Find the one that *you* were called to stand for. So, I'll ask the question again: What would you march in the streets for? Maybe multiple issues could get you out early on a Saturday morning to march, which is great! The problem comes when a person cannot identify any one thing they would march for (and I mean "march" in a metaphorical way).

If you're struggling to determine what you stand for or against, start thinking about what tugs at your heart. Maybe you have an emotional reaction when you watch a Feed the Children commercial, but feel nothing when you see a PETA ad. Or maybe you feel guilty every time you don't stop to help a homeless person. Think about what the little voice in your head keeps hinting that you should be doing more about. The one thing you keep coming back to. The one topic that could get you worked up in a conversation with friends.

Once you determine what you stand for and against, home in on those issues. This will allow you to give back to your community and also prevent you from spreading yourself too thin, by fighting a fight that was never yours to fight.

What do you enjoy? In 2018, I turned thirty. I remember putting together a highlight video of year twenty-nine and all I had accomplished. After watching the final video, I couldn't believe how much I had done in 365 days. I had gone with a client to *The Ellen DeGeneres Show,* I had my first top one hundred NFL Draft pick, I signed the number one overall softball pick, I attended the ESPYs, I successfully pitched my client and got her on the cover of *ESPN: The Body Issue,* I shot a pilot for a TV show that was all about me, I started working for Lil Wayne, I was named an NAACP Millennial Trailblazer, I won Woman of the Year, and I gave the commencement speech at my alma mater, Booker T. Washington High School. Wow. What a year. As I sat there and reflected on how much I'd succeeded in year twenty-nine, I was shocked.

I wasn't shocked because I'd done so much—I was shocked because I didn't feel like I'd done much of anything. In year twenty-nine, I'd struggled with internal happiness more than I have in my entire life. Yet year twenty-nine also was my most successful year thus far. What I learned is that success doesn't always equate to happiness or joy.

Therefore, when you're crafting your "me statement," don't overlook this important part: the things you enjoy. As weird as it may sound, finding things I truly enjoy was the hardest part of completing my "me statement." The things you enjoy are indicative of who you are. If you enjoy skydiving and rock climbing, you're likely adventurous—that is a part of who you are. If you enjoy watching movies and cooking at home, you may be a homebody—that is a part of who you are. Step away from the noise and take a breather, so you can determine what truly makes you happy. Whether it's an activity, personal time, or something totally different, whatever it is, it plays an instrumental part in you being your authentic self.

What do you want your legacy to be? The last part of who you are is your legacy, which this quote from the musical *Hamilton* defines brilliantly: "It's planting seeds in a garden you never get to see."[1] Those seeds, whether good or bad, will eventually grow and become your legacy. They're planted so the people who come after you can enjoy the fruits of your labor when you're no longer here.

Think of people throughout history who have had a long-lasting influence on those around them and on future generations—people like Martin Luther King Jr., Nelson Mandela, and Mother Teresa. When you think of these people, you're thinking of the legacy they built and the reputation they established for themselves. You probably don't know many, if any, minor details about them or the seeds they planted along the way, but their names are recognized around the world, and their legacies have far outlasted their time on Earth.

A legacy can be tangible, such as money or land. It also can be intangible, such as passing down family traditions or instilling faith and religion in your children. When you consider your legacy, think of what you want to be remembered for. What contribution do you plan to make to future generations—to your kids, your family, and this world? How do you want to influence those around you? What impact do you want to have, and what work will it take to accomplish this? You can also think of your legacy as your ministry. It's your ultimate purpose.

At the end of your life, people won't remember your résumé, your accomplishments, or your net worth. However, they'll remember how you made them feel and how you impacted their lives. When you leave this earth, plan to leave it better than you found it. That's what a legacy looks like.

If something doesn't align with who I am—that is, with my identity, beliefs, stance, enjoyment, and legacy—it isn't guaranteed my extra time, money, energy, or concern. Do yourself a favor: commit to taking the journey of determining who you are and make a pledge that, every single day, you'll be your true and authentic self.

AGENT YOU: TAKE ACTION!

1. Your "me statement" is a critical part of being your authentic self. This statement covers five areas: identity, belief, stance, enjoyment, and legacy. To assess each of these areas, ask yourself the following questions:

   • Identity: How do you view yourself? List the primary ways.
   • Belief: What are your core values? If you're struggling to come up with ideas, an online search will point you toward dozens of websites that provides lists you can choose from.
   • Stance: What cause would you march in the streets to support? Even if you'd support multiple causes in this way, if you could only choose one, what would it be?
   • Enjoyment: What activities make you happy? If you're like me and have trouble pinpointing things you enjoy, try to remember times when you've smiled and laughed a lot, and what you were doing then.
   • Legacy: If you could choose one thing for people to remember about you after you die, what would it be? Keep in mind that this can be something close to home, such as "I want people to remember that I loved my family," or something broader, such as "I want people to remember that I fought for global women's rights to education."

You—and only
you—determine
your authentic self.

CHAPTER FOUR

Treat Yourself Like the Brand You Are

The Netflix show *All American* is one of my favorites. One night I was watching the premiere of season two, and the craziest thing happened. In the episode, a girl walks up to the main character, a high school football player, and introduces herself as a football guru. The main character responds, "Sounds like another Nicole Lynn in the making."

What!?

I fell out of my seat. Was I hearing things? Did the main character just say my name on TV? I couldn't believe it. They were referring to me as a sports agent—they were referring to me as a household name! In the midst of my surprise and excitement, I realized I'd successfully done what I set out to do: build a brand.

It was almost five years into my profession before I learned that I—little old me, someone no one is worried about—am a brand. I didn't understand the concept of branding myself, because I thought branding was for models, actors, and influencers. However, everyone is a brand, no matter their profession. Yes, you heard me right. Doctors are brands. Lawyers are brands. Teachers are brands. And, obviously, entrepreneurs are brands.

You are a brand, and you should be showcasing your brand every chance you get.

The power of your brand should be so strong that it precedes you. Before you even walk into a room, the people in the room should have an idea about who you are, what you are about, and why you are credible. Your brand should show up in place of you. Your brand should be so powerful that people believe they know you at a deeply personal level, when in reality they only know the brand. Even more, when the person and brand are so intertwined that others don't see a difference between the two, you know your mission is accomplished.

You will never be the best business owner, influencer, motivational speaker, and so on if you don't focus and truly home in on building out your brand. Think about the most successful companies in the world, each of which has a clearly identifiable and memorable brand. These companies have trained their customer bases to think of the company when the brand is mentioned. For example, when you think of "golden arches," you absolutely think of McDonald's. When you hear the phrase "Just do it," what's your first thought? Nike. These brands are so powerful that consumers are unable to separate the brand from the product.

One day, I was talking brands with a friend, Marquay Baul, who's a top financial adviser in the NFL world. He asked me, "What's that item called that you use to blow your nose with?"

I answered confidently and without missing a beat: "Kleenex."

"Wrong," he said. "What you use to blow your nose with is facial tissue. Kleenex is just the brand name."

I was shocked, but he was right. I thought about it for a minute: Well, I wouldn't say, "I need some Crest to brush my teeth." I'm more likely to say, "I need some toothpaste." But with facial tissue, my immediate instinct was to say Kleenex. The reason? Kleenex has created such a powerful brand that you're unable to disassociate it from the product. The brand is so influential that it overpowers not only the specific product, but competing products too. It is not surprising that I can't name a single facial tissue company besides Kleenex, although I'm sure they're out there. That is what brand power looks like.

When I first got certified as a sports agent, I wasn't big into social media. I didn't even use my Instagram account. I reached out to a publicist friend and pitched a crazy idea to her: I wanted to build a brand as a sports agent that could help me recruit athletes, and influence and motivate other women who wanted to get into the sports industry. And I wanted to do this solely through social media, which I'd never seen done in my field. At the time, few agents even had Instagram pages, so this was absolutely outside the norm. But I knew I was different, and I wasn't into following norms anyway. I didn't care what other agents were doing, because, honey, I wasn't "other agents"—I was Agent Nicole Lynn in the making.

When building a brand, do not lose sight of the goal: you want people to immediately think of *you* when they think of a particular service or product, just like we naturally think of Kleenex. I knew that even though hundreds of certified sports agents are out there, most people couldn't name a single sports agent besides the fictional sports agent Jerry Maguire. What this told me was that these other agents didn't have brands. I decided that I wanted my name and my face to be the first thing that comes to mind when someone thinks "sports agent."

This should be your goal too. You want to be a household name. When someone needs a real estate agent, a wedding planner, a stylist, a baker, or whatever your profession may be, your name should be the first one that comes to mind. And until that happens, you have work to do.

DEFINING YOUR BRAND: CHOOSING YOUR PILLARS

When you start to get serious about your brand, you must decide what you want people to think of when they think of you. I call these your pillars. Let's use basketball player Steph Curry as an example. When you think of Steph Curry, what are the first things that come to mind? For me, it's basketball/three-pointers, his faith in God, and his wife, Ayesha Curry. When you think of Steph, do you think of those same things? I bet you do, because those are Steph's pillars. Steph has quietly built a brand with three pillars: basketball, faith, and family. Everything Steph does, whether an endorsement deal or a social media post, almost always seems to align with these pillars. Steph's brand is so strong that it's typically intertwined with the product (him).

Brands need to be specific and narrow. Therefore, the pillars that define your brand should be clear. For my brand, I wanted people to see a black woman who was staying true to herself while navigating the world of sports. I also wanted them to see a woman they could relate to, learn from, follow, and see as a mentor. Thus my brand pillars are sports, inspiration, mentorship, and empowering women.

To establish my pillars, I needed to be vulnerable and transparent in my posts. I shared my failures for the entire world to see. I also continued to post tips on how to get into the business, because I wanted to use my brand as a platform to help others. Last, I wanted my brand to ignite a yearning for people to walk in their purpose. So, I posted about purpose and following your dreams. Anything outside of the above rarely found its way to my page. I wanted to make sure my followers got consistency, and they were getting the posts they signed up for. I never wanted my brand to surround family or friends or anything tied to my personal life, which was strategic. So, unless you truly know me, you're unlikely to know much about the people closest to me, since they're typically not shown on my page or throughout my brand.

After you choose your pillars, you should be married to them. Anything that doesn't fit within your pillars shouldn't show up or attempt to creep into your brand. Your followers/customers/fan base thrive on consistency. They sign up to support you based on your pillars, and when you change these, you'll likely lose followers. This doesn't mean you can't evolve or change your brand, but when you do so, you must be strategic about how that happens. If you're planning a brand change, don't do it all at once. Ease your followers into the change by exposing them to new pillars drop by drop, as you make small, deliberate changes.

The more consistent you are with your pillars and pushing your brand into the world, the bigger your brand will grow. I knew that my plan to build a brand as a sports agent was working when I went places and people would address me by my brand: "Hey, you're Agent Nicole Lynn." Of course, my birth name does not have "agent" in it, but I had effectively built my brand, so it was hard for people to associate me with anything beyond the brand.

If you already have a brand and people mention your brand when they describe you, you've done it right. Oh, that's Ashley, the girl who sells weave. That's Taylor, the stylist. Oh, that's Lauren, the girl who can dress. That's Meredith, the middle school teacher. Many of you may have organically built your brand and are seeing the fruits of it right now, but if you haven't, this next section is for you.

HOW TO BUILD A BRAND

Let's talk about how to go about building this brand. While I'm not some kind of marketing guru, I've built and assisted in building several brands for athletes, celebrities, and myself. I've seen what works and what doesn't. This chapter is by no means an in-depth analysis on branding, but I hope to give you a high-level view of what building a brand looks like.

Building a brand doesn't have to be difficult or expensive. I recommend starting with the basics. As stated above, first you need to define your brand and decide on your pillars.

Everything you do from this point forward should specifically align with your pillars.

After you have your pillars in place, decide what your brand's overall theme will be. What do you want people to think of when they think of your brand? If your brand surrounds selling clothing, maybe the theme is affordable quality. If your brand is surrounding you as a personal trainer, maybe the theme is weight loss. If you're an influencer, maybe your theme is social activism. Your pillars should help your consumer base and following recognize the overall theme. Thus, when a consumer is thinking of a product or service, you want them to immediately think of you because you're a household name, while simultaneously thinking of your theme. Let me give you an example: Someone is planning a fancy wedding. They immediately think of you, the wedding planner, because you're a household name when it comes to weddings, and they think of your theme, which happens to be luxury weddings.

Now that you've identified your pillars and theme, it's time to determine your audience.

Every brand has a different audience, and knowing your audience will help dictate how to get your brand out there. When I first started building my brand, I focused on having a better social media presence. I prioritized Instagram because, based on my age, I knew many of the people I wanted to reach were on that platform. I started posting more consistently and made my content specific to my pillars, especially sports. I also utilized hashtags that aligned with my pillars. The more I posted and the more consistent I became, the more my following grew.

There are many different mediums to get your brand out there, and that's where marketing comes in. Building a brand is different than marketing that brand. I recommend you focus on building, then hire a professional to assist in marketing.

Building a brand in an industry where personal brands are uncommon didn't come without backlash. I remember how much my social media activity bothered many of my peer agents. They saw my posts as self-serving and all about me. Well, funny enough, they were right. *Social media is all about you.* Social media is a place for you to advocate for yourself, to sell your skills, and to showcase who you are.

Although I knew social media was important for my brand, their comments still hurt. Every time I posted something, my stomach dropped. *Were they going to text me or make a comment about it?* In spite of the negative comments, I kept pushing and creating content that no other sports agent had done before. Six years later, I now see many of my peer agents with active social media platforms similar to mine. I like to believe I was a trailblazer in this respect, and seeing others—who once vehemently opposed what I was doing—do it as well shows me I was on to something.

Building a brand isn't just for fun. The ultimate goal is that your successful brand will translate to furthering your purpose. Whether you're hoping that your brand gets more people to buy your products or for more people to choose you for a specific service, either way, it all boils down to the bottom line. When I started building my brand, clients reached out to me based solely on what they saw on my social media. Funny enough, five of my current clients found me on social media and sent me a direct message. My plan was working. My brand was bringing in new business.

Because I was getting so much traction on my social media from potential clients, I then built a website, where people could go to read more information about me. My website and my social media have a consistent theme. Just like my social media, you won't find anything on my website that's inconsistent with my pillars. Your social media and website also should be in complete alignment.

HAVING A BRAND IN THE WORKPLACE

Just like you build a brand for a company, you should have a personal brand in the workplace. Essentially, your brand at work is your professional reputation—the way coworkers and peers view you as an employee. Does your brand represent a person who is always late? Someone who doesn't turn down assignments? Or are you the working mom? The way you carry yourself to the way you do business are all pieces that make up your professional workplace brand.

My professional reputation includes being someone who is a hard worker, a team player, and authentic.

One of the most important things you can do while building a brand at work is to be your authentic self. I know how clichéd this may sound, but remember why the company hired you. They hired you not just for your work ethic and résumé, but because of your individuality and who you are as a person. When hiring managers place comparable résumés next to one another, they make hiring decisions based on which candidate is the best fit for the culture. When the company hired you, they kept this in mind. They didn't look to hire someone who comes to work and blends in. The secret sauce is *you*—so be you every single day.

Do Not "Cover"

When talking about building a workplace brand, I feel it's necessary to discuss *covering*. The act of covering is when someone silences personal characteristics to fit in with the dominant personality or culture of an organization.[1] It's common for people—whether minorities, women, or any other nondominant group—to cover in the workplace in an effort to fit in and, more important, to make others feel more comfortable around them.

During my tenure in corporate America, I find that, more often than not, minorities cover. An example of covering would be changing your hair or the clothes you wear to conform to what your coworkers are used to. Another example of covering is using a different tone of voice, word choice, or code-switching (switching among dialects, styles, or registers when speaking) when at work.[2] You're also covering when you hide important details about your life, because you assume your coworkers couldn't understand or relate. Covering can be very dangerous.

In the workplace, I do not cover. People who cover put those who come after them at a disadvantage. When someone covers, they're often doing so with the goal of making people feel comfortable around them. But instead of making others feel comfortable by conforming to who *they* are, why don't we teach them to be comfortable with who *we* are?

I believe there are many people who have never worked in a professional setting with a black person. Not that they've never met a black person or been friends with a black person—but that they have never worked with one. Statistics show us that corporate America is not diverse. For instance, only 5 percent of lawyers identify as African American. Because nonminorities in the workplace are used to being around people who look like them, they're usually not familiar with how minorities act/dress/talk/look in corporate America.

Therefore, instead of hiding behind social norms, I make a conscious effort to be myself. I feel that by choosing to be who God created me to be, I get the chance to educate the people around me about my culture.

For example, I, like many black women, love the versatility of being able to change my hair. Some days I wear short, jet-black hair, other days I'm in braids, and on occasion you may catch me in twenty-two-inch blond weave. I also sometimes choose to wear my hair in its natural state. In corporate America, I've noticed that many black women are afraid to change their hair. One of my black coworkers once told me she was hesitant to get braids before a beach vacation because she was afraid of what people might say.

I remember the first time I decided to wear my blond wig to work. I wore it on a Tuesday and was over it within forty-eight hours, so I reverted to my normal black hair by Friday. One of the white lawyers at my law firm asked if my hair was "a weave." Instead of getting frustrated with him, I recognized his ignorance and took the opportunity to educate him. After all, this could have been the first time he'd seen a woman in weave.

I said: "Yes, this is weave. I am only telling you this because we are friends. But I want you to know that you should never, ever ask a black girl that question again."

He was shook. He asked why.

I told him this was one of those things he just had to trust me on. "I recognize that you probably haven't worked with a black woman before, but asking a black woman about her hair is totally off limits." I didn't sister girl him, and I wasn't rude—I took a moment to teach him and help mitigate his ignorance.

Imagine if I'd been covering. This man might have gone through the rest of his life without understanding that black women wear weave, and that it's rude to ask them about it. Although I may have been uncomfortable for a few moments, it was worth it because I eliminated a small portion of ignorance for the black girls who come after me.

One time I attended a women's event, and the speaker told the attendees that if they ever have to leave work for their children, just say, "I have a prior engagement." Never reference your kids unless you want to be known as the "office working mom." In the moment, I thought that was great advice. Looking back, I realize how dangerous this type of advice can be. If every woman hides her motherhood at work, working moms will never be normalized. More to the point, if being a mom is a part of who you are, it should be valued, not hidden.

Other examples of covering include the following:

- A Muslim woman is invited to lunch during Ramadan but declines, saying she has a doctor's appointment. In reality, she is fasting as part of her religious practice and doesn't want to tell her coworkers.
- A Jewish man requests a vacation day at work to go to the beach, but he's really attending services for a religious holiday.
- A black girl straightens her hair for work because she's afraid to wear her natural curl pattern in front of her coworkers.

- A young woman barely able to pay her bills puts herself deep into debt to purchase expensive outfits and accessories to wear to work because she's afraid of being judged for her clothes.

In these situations, each individual is covering. They're managing their identity and only revealing the pieces of it that they believe others will be comfortable with. When you decide not to cover, at first this may result in some awkward conversations. But I believe there's nothing wrong with helping someone who is innocently ignorant learn and perhaps understand something about me or my culture. However, this help shouldn't be confused with trying to teach someone you've already had a conversation with or someone who is intentionally unwelcoming of who you are.

I challenge you to stop covering in the workplace. If you want to reach your full potential, you have to be okay with being different. The most successful business professionals aren't concerned about being the only minority, woman, or person of a specific faith in the room. They embrace who they are and compel others to do the same.

Let's create workplaces where people can come as they are. Where everyone is accepting of another's differences and realizes that differences are what make an organization great. Diversity is crucial in the workplace, and differences are the heart of diversity. And if an organization doesn't believe in this school of thought, perhaps it isn't the place for you.

When you decide what type of workplace reputation and brand you want, make sure it includes you being *you*.

AGENT YOU:
TAKE ACTION!

1. Ask yourself: "How do I envision my brand?" One helpful way to answer this question is to fill in the blank. For instance, I am often referred to by my brand and my name: Agent Nicole Lynn. Who do you want to be known as? _____

2. Take steps to build your brand. Even if you've already begun the process of building your brand, now is a good time to evaluate the work you've already done and make sure you haven't gotten off track along the way.

   - Choose your pillars. What do you want people to think of when they think of you?
   - Choose your theme. What do you want people to think of when they think of your brand?
   - Identify your audience. Who is your brand intended to reach and help?
   - Choose your medium. Where are you most likely to engage your audience?
   - Be consistent. Across all your platforms, make sure that all the content relates to at least one of your pillars, adheres to your theme, will appeal to your audience, and is appropriate for the medium.

3. Make every effort not to cover. Most of us fall victim to covering in one way or another, whether

in the workplace or elsewhere. Evaluate the things about yourself or your life that you've withheld from others. Are you keeping those things under wraps because of fear or a desire to make sure others are comfortable? If you're covering in any way, list at least two or three ways you, those around you, or those who come after you can benefit from your refusal to cover.

No matter who you are,
you are a brand.

CHAPTER FIVE

Embrace a
Mamba Mentality

As much as I preach on walking in purpose and achieving your goals, I'd be remiss if I didn't write about what comes along with that: sacrifice. When you're all in on pursuing a dream, there will be long days and longer nights. There will be sleep deprivation and missed events. There will be things you sacrifice by choice, and things you sacrifice against your will. The most successful people in the world are the same people who are willing to make sacrifices.

The question I'm asked more than any other is, "How do you do it all?" This question makes me extremely uncomfortable. In an effort to avoid this conversation, when someone asks me what I do for a living, I hesitate. Depending on the environment, I tell them I'm a lawyer, or I tell them I'm a sports agent. I rarely tell them both for a few reasons. If I tell them both, someone always assumes that my sports job is *a* side hustle—it is not. And then I find myself having to explain how much work is involved in my full-time sports gig. Also, when I tell people I'm a sports agent, that revelation tends to dominate the conversation, and I hate that. Imagine being at a networking event with ten people in a circle and all the focus is on you. Finally, I am embarrassed to say that, here I am, five years later, still working two full-time jobs. I'm not proud of the amount I work—there's nothing sexy about being busy all the time.

If I were truthful when asked how I do it all, my answer would be that I juggle two full-time careers. I work sixty to ninety hours a week as a lawyer for a big international law firm while also working nonstop as a full-time sports agent. My law job and my sports agent work don't overlap whatsoever, and neither is a side hustle.

Here's a glimpse into my typical week: Monday through Friday, I'm in the law office, writing motions and preparing for trial. However, that doesn't stop at 5:00 p.m. Working for a large law firm means always being available to partners and working late nights and many weekends. It also includes attending firm events, serving on the hiring committee, and being a "good firm citizen." It's a nonstop gig.

On the weekend, I'm likely flying somewhere for my sports job. Saturday, I'll travel to a college football game to watch a recruit and, I hope, catch him after the game for a short introduction. Sunday morning, I fly to any of the numerous NFL cities to watch my clients play or to sit with them for a two-hour dinner to get face time. Monday mornings are the absolute worst. I usually catch a 5:00 a.m. flight from whatever NFL city I'm in back to Houston and walk straight into my law office at 9:00 a.m. While working in law during the week, I'm also constantly handling my athlete clients' business: putting out fires, negotiating contracts, dealing with family drama, booking flights, running errands, planning vacations, and so on.

So . . . how do I do it? Sometimes I ask myself that, and even I'm still not sure how I pull it off. First, instead of taking annual vacations, I use any and all of the vacation time I have at my law firm to attend the NFL Scouting Combine, NFL Senior Bowl, and NFL Draft. Since my vacation days are used for sports, most years I have no "baecations" and few girls' trips, and self-care is out the window. Second, I am always "on."

Unless you're someone who's always "on," this tendency can be hard to understand. Being always "on" means you're available to work at any moment. Your phone is never on silent mode. You're willing to leave dinner or a movie or even walk outside in the middle of a wedding ceremony to take a client call. You don't take days off, and when you do anything that doesn't involve work, you still find a way to sneak work in.

SUCCESS ISN'T ALWAYS PRETTY

It's important that I emphasize this because I never want to give anyone a false sense of reality. Even though my Instagram is littered with photos of me attending movie premieres and on the field at NFL games, I want to paint an honest picture. Because I'm stubborn and work two full-time jobs (while writing a book, producing a show, oh, and being human), I must sacrifice things that are important to me. I've learned that my core values begin with my career (not something I'm proud of), so my sacrifices aren't made in that area of life. Instead, my sacrifices are usually in my personal life.

Even over the past year, I've had to sacrifice taking care of my health. I'm unable to work out consistently, and because I live on a plane, I often eat out. In the past couple of years, I've gained more than thirty pounds—that's right, thirty pounds. And my doctor tells me that my blood pressure is way too high for my age and that something has to be done. Yet here I am, working and working and not doing a thing about it. I sacrifice eight hours of sleep a night. I don't remember the last time I slept through the night. I toss and turn and wake up over and over again because my to-do list is always running through my head. It's torture, really. I sacrifice time with the people I love, including my husband, Gabe. I sacrifice having a family. (I've been married for nine years and I grew up wanting to have kids. But every time the thought of kids comes up, I panic. Where would I find the time?) I sacrifice rest, I sacrifice eating home-cooked meals, and I sacrifice alone time. More than any single thing, I sacrifice my peace. Anxiety attacks and sadness out of nowhere have become part of my norm. Regardless, I put on a face and keep it moving. This is the price I have paid, and continue to pay, for success. And do not be fooled: it's a hefty price.

If anyone tries to tell you that success can come without any sacrifice at all, *run!* They're not only being dishonest but setting you up for failure. Did you know that only 20 percent of millionaires inherited their wealth?[1] That means 80 percent of millionaires are self-made. I can assure you that, out of that 80 percent, few of those people are average. Excluding lottery winners, I'd bet you that very few of those millionaires work normal nine-to-five jobs, come home at a decent hour to make dinner, work out three times a week, and enjoy their weekend with some "me" time. Those millionaires are the people who will sacrifice their personal lives, their peace of mind, their sleep, their bodies, and sometimes something greater, to get to where they are.

Maybe you're hoping you'll get lucky and become an overnight success. We've all seen it happen. A YouTuber, a vlogger, a rapper, a comedian—one day a nobody and the next day a viral video becomes a claim to fame. But are these people truly overnight successes? For example, let's take Tiffany Haddish. You can't turn on a TV without seeing her. In the past couple of years, Tiffany was a guest on *The Ellen DeGeneres Show,* met Oprah, starred in several major feature films, and had her own stand-up comedy special. But where in the world did she come from? On the outside looking in, she had a role in the movie *Girls Trip,* and *bam!* was an overnight success.

However, her success was anything but "overnight." Haddish worked in Hollywood for several years before her hard work was recognized. Although it looked like she came out of nowhere, she was doing everything necessary to reach her goals. She had a goal, she had direction, she put in the work, and she took calculated risks.

When you see "overnight success" stories, know that their hard work likely had been done in private long before the person was acknowledged in public. In short, there is no such thing as an overnight success. To paraphrase a popular quote: *Most successful people get to places in their life that others will never reach because they're willing to do things that others will never do.*[2]

I'm not trying to discourage you here. I'm just trying to give you a glimpse into how a life of success could look.

Another example of a successful person who worked hard behind the scenes is Kobe Bryant (may he rest in peace). One of the best ever basketball players, he took his job as a player seriously. When playing for Team USA in the Olympics, he arrived three hours before his peers every single practice. This means he arrived at the facility at 4:00 a.m. and had completed three hours of drills and a workout before his teammates even woke up. He also was the last person to leave the gym each day. Outsiders looking in called him crazy; he called it the "mamba mentality." People who are serious about their goals will do anything to reach them. That includes sometimes making the ultimate sacrifices.

I'll say it again: a life of success isn't always pretty. Most people only see the end product, when in reality hundreds of hours have gone into what they now see. Corey Wilson, a former football player for the University of Oklahoma, whose career was cut short after a car accident paralyzed him from the waist down, still always asks, "Do you want to be good or great?" Being great instead of good is as simple as warming up your day-old pizza in the oven instead of the microwave. Take no shortcuts on your journey to success.

When working toward becoming successful, the question isn't whether you have what it takes. You probably do. The question is whether you'll do what it takes. That answer to the latter isn't always clear.

Ask yourself right now: "Do I have what it takes?" If you answer yes, then ask yourself, "Will I do what it takes?" As you're deciding whether or not this hustle life is for you, let me make something clear: this type of sacrifice isn't for everyone. And there's nothing wrong with deciding something isn't for you.

Because I feel it's important to be transparent, through-out this book I've described what my journey to success has looked like. For some of you, this information excites you and makes you want to go harder. Others might be thinking, *You do you, but that's not how I want to live my life.* And either path is fine, as long as you're living true to yourself and your values.

USE WHAT YOU HAVE

This seems like a good time to point out that while most people have to make sacrifices on their journey to success, those sacrifices aren't necessarily equal. A popular quote states, "You have the same twenty-four hours as Beyoncé." This may be one of the most misleading quotes on the face of the earth (and this is coming from me, the "president" of the Beyhive). Yes, you have the same twenty-four hours, but do you have the same twenty-four-hours' worth of resources? Likely not.

I don't have Beyoncé-level resources, but I can afford certain things that make my hard work easier. For example, I have a cleaning lady who cleans and unpacks after I travel. I don't have time to cook, but I can afford to eat whatever, whenever. I can afford first-class tickets to make flying easier, and so I can work while flying. I can afford a virtual assistant who keeps my life in order for all things sports. Although my life is extremely stressful, money isn't one of those stressors. And anyone who knows my story understands this hasn't always been the case.

So, in hearing success stories—like Kobe's, like Beyoncé's, like mine—remember that it can be productive and motivating to compare your hustle and your hard work, but don't lose sight of the resources that give others an advantage: for instance, Kobe's private gym, Beyoncé's in-home recording studio, or my personal assistant.

One of my favorite books is *Lean In: Women, Work, and the Will to Lead* by Sheryl Sandberg. Sandberg is the COO (chief operating officer) of Facebook and an HBIC (head B in charge) if there ever was one. In Sandberg's book, she talks a lot about how she got where she is, while also reminding the reader that she's a millionaire and has triple the help of a normal human being. I applaud Sandberg and others who are honest about their above-average resources.

What if you don't have Sandberg's resources but want to get to her level? *Work with what you have.* I didn't always have my current means, but I found a way. At one time I couldn't afford to buy a nice suit for my client-recruiting meetings. I bought a cheap blazer and Forever 21 dress pants, and wore the same things to every client meeting. This repetition made the outfit seem like my "uniform." Taking flights used to be beyond my budget, so I drove everywhere and made a fire Beyoncé playlist, which helped me endure even the twelve-hour car rides.

Get creative in your pursuit of success. For every rich-kid, trust-fund millionaire story, a rags-to-riches story sits right next to it. In other words, people who came from nothing all across the globe have found success with little means, time, and money. If you do what you can with what you have, it will get done.

ONLY YOU CAN DEFINE SUCCESS

It's also important to remember that success is defined by *you*. It's not defined by society's standards, social media, or books on success—like this one. Success is subjective. Success for you may mean having two beautiful babies and being the best stay-at-home mom or dad the world has ever seen. Success could mean staying in a nine-to-five job and moving up the corporate ladder one position at a time. For others, success is simply living life with indescribable peace.

In your search for purpose, you also need to define what success looks like. When each individual decides what success looks like, he or she can then act according to that vision. If my purpose in life is to be a sports agent, and I become a sports agent, does that mean I'm successful? It might. But even in the realm of sports agents, success has different meanings. Some sports agents deem success as having X number of clients. Others deem success as having a certain level of draft pick.

Finding your purpose is one struggle, but defining what success means for you is a whole different process. Take a minute and decide what a life full of purpose means to you. Then consider how you define success. I challenge you to write this down right now: I consider success to be _____.

You can't be successful when you don't even know what success looks like for you. Here is how I define success for myself: I consider success to be . . .

- financially able to survive with one career
- representing top athletes around the world

- having players come to me, instead of recruiting them
- an expert in my field, but someone who's always open to learning
- prioritizing my marriage and family above my career
- making millions of dollars so I can give most of it away
- having indescribable peace through it all

My version of success is specific to my life, core values, intrinsic needs, and God-given purpose. It's also tied to what makes me feel worthy and, most important, what gives me joy. Once you achieve certain milestones or recognize you're unwilling to make certain sacrifices, your definition of success might change. And that's healthy and appropriate. Your life should be lived in accordance with your beliefs—not someone else's.

AGENT YOU:
TAKE ACTION!

1. Keep in mind that success isn't always pretty. You most likely have what it takes to succeed, but are you willing to do what it takes to succeed?

   - What are you willing to sacrifice to achieve your desired success? A long-term relationship? Financial security? Sleep?
   - What are you unwilling to sacrifice? These are your nonnegotiables, which can help you eliminate options along your journey to success.

Sometimes it's equally important to know what you aren't willing to do as it is to know what you are willing to do.

2. Use what you have. We all have finite resources, and some of us have access to more resources than others.

- Make a list of the things you think you need to succeed (e.g., more time, a degree, a part-time assistant).
- Do you currently have all these resources? If not, how can you secure them? Or do you already have something that can serve as a substitute for the time being? For instance, if you need more time but can't afford childcare, maybe you could offer one of your skills in exchange for a friend watching your kid(s) for a few hours a week.

3. Define success on your terms. Complete this sentence: I consider success to be _____.

Only you can
define what success
looks like for *you*.

CHAPTER SIX

Stay Ready, So You Don't Have to Get Ready

One of my lifelong career goals is to become a contributor for a major TV network, like ESPN. In the perfect world, this is how I've always envisioned my career: major sports agent who reps some of the biggest athletes in the world, author, speaker, and contributor/analyst on a major sports network several times a year. When it came to being a TV analyst, I had no idea where to start, and at one point I even considered hiring a media agent. (How funny is that—an agent, hiring an agent? *Spoiler alert:* I am now a media agent myself, because, why not?) I decided to reach out to some of my reporter friends for some insight. Oddly enough, I was hesitant to tell anyone about this goal because

I was a little nervous I wouldn't be taken seriously. (Can you relate?) I also didn't want to come off as condescending by asking how to get into TV, since I had zero experience and no relevant schooling. I kept imagining a reporter thinking, *Who does she think she is that she can just up and do my job? It took me fifteen years to get where I am.*

With all this going through my mind, and my insecurities, I reached out to a trusted friend and asked her what to do. Her advice was to create a reel tape—a video with short clips of me in front of a camera, to prove that I could do the job. Ideally, a reel tape highlights broadcasters in different news settings to demonstrate their versatility and so forth. I obviously had no recordings of me in a broadcast or analyst role, so my friend recommended I create fake news, to show how I perform on camera.

This didn't sound too hard. I could ask a friend to record me talking in front of a green screen and edit it, so the footage would flow. Perfect. I had my plan and was ready to create my tape so I could start pitching myself.

Then life happened.

Have you ever had the best intentions to do something, but never got around to it? <Raises hand.> Guilty as charged.

Fast-forward to three months later. I was at the Ravens versus Raiders game, supporting my NFL clients. My husband, Gabe, had played football with a Baltimore Ravens player and was offered suite tickets. We were grateful for the suite tickets because Baltimore is notoriously cold in the winter, and it had been raining all week. When visiting my players, I usually sit outside in the family section, but for the football stadiums that aren't covered, winter can be tough because you're outside in the elements.

As we headed to the suite, we were told the player shared the suite with someone else. So, when we arrived, we expected to be around people we didn't know, which was fine with us.

We walked into the suite and introduced ourselves to the new faces. The last person I approached was a beautiful black woman with curly, honey-colored hair and the most gorgeous smile. When I went to shake her hand, I realized I'd met her before: at the ESPY awards just a few months prior, when I'd accompanied my client on the red carpet. What I remembered about that interaction was that I'd been escorting my client into an exclusive area at the ESPYs, just as someone else was escorting this woman. She was obviously important, but I didn't think much of it at the time.

"Did we meet briefly at the ESPYs?" she asked. What were the odds that I'd met this woman in Los Angeles a few months earlier, and now we were on the other side of the country in a ten-person suite, meeting again?

I then received a text from my husband, who was on the other side of the suite: "That is Sage Steele, the big-time analyst for ESPN."

Let me pause and tell you how amazing my husband is. Anyone who knows me knows I have zero facial recognition. This has been a big hurdle for me in my career. I can't tell you how many times I've been standing next to, or even talking to, Chris Rock, Spike Lee, LeToya Luckett, 2 Chainz, and others, and I had no idea who they were. It even happens with athletes. I'll never forget when I thought Tim Tebow was Tom Brady, and I introduced him as such.

How do I work in sports and entertainment when I can't recognize famous faces, you might wonder. Because I have ride-or-die friends and family who help a sister out.

Okay, back to the story.

My husband, knowing my weakness, sent me this text as an FYI, because without me even saying it, he knew I didn't recognize her. Can we agree this man is the real MVP?

So there I was, about to watch this game with Sage Steele and sit in the suite with her for *four uninterrupted hours.* I immediately thought about my goal to be a TV sports analyst. I contemplated asking her for advice about how to break into the business, but I second-guessed myself. *She probably gets this all the time,* I thought. *Why would she ever want to help me? She doesn't even know me.*

I left the suite and walked around the club area of the stadium to clear my head. I told myself that I was in the room with someone who potentially could help make my dream come true, just by making an introduction for me. I reminded myself that I'd gotten to this place in my life by consistently pushing myself outside my comfort zone and by taking a shot. I also reminded myself that the worst she could do was say no. *Listen, you aren't asking for a kidney here. You are asking for ten minutes of advice—that's it. You can do this.*

Have you ever been in this situation? You know someone who has a connection that could be beneficial to your dream, but something got in the way of you asking for help? We all do it! Let me remind you of the famous and very overused quote: "You miss 100 percent of the shots you don't take." Many times, the reason we don't take the shot is because of fear. Fear of rejection, fear of embarrassment, fear of being unqualified, fear of being unworthy.

Listen here, sis: *There is absolutely nothing wrong with being afraid.* If I said I was never afraid, I'd be lying. Fear only becomes a problem when you let it dictate your steps and hold you back from an opportunity. If there were some magic recipe for success, I'm sure it would include these ingredients: a cup of hard work, a sprinkle of talent, two big scoops of the favor of God, and a tablespoon of fear.

Would you believe me if I told you that fear can be a good thing? Well, it can. It pushes humans beyond the bounds of their comfort zone, and in this process, we're molded into the people we're meant to be. It's hard to become our true, successful selves when we've never taken risks and never been afraid.

The next time you're faced with fear, take a moment to appreciate it. Will you let fear hinder you, or will fear become the conduit for something greater?

I've often faced fear in my professional life. I was afraid to approach certain players, many of whom are now my clients. I was afraid to ask my law firm to allow me to have a side hustle in sports, which they approved. And I was afraid to approach Sage Steele in a football suite. Pushing through the fear was critical for me to get where I am. I recognized it was there, I understood it was healthy, and I used the fear as a stepping-stone to get to the other side.

Taking my own advice, I decided this was a once-in-a-lifetime opportunity and I wouldn't let it pass me by. *Put me in, Coach—I'm ready.*

I finally mustered the confidence to tell her my ultimate goal and ask for some much-needed advice. To my surprise, she was super receptive. She told me she thought it was a great idea and, funny enough, the timing was perfect, based on what was happening at the network. She asked if I could send her my reel tape the next day, so she could send it to a talent director at a major network.

My stomach dropped. Reel tape? Oh no, the *reel tape*! You know, the video I was supposed to create months earlier, and

I had all the best intentions to do so but never got around to it. Over and over, I kept putting it on the back burner. And, of course, I never could have imagined that I'd end up needing one that fast.

I learned a hard life lesson that day, something I know and preach, but didn't act on: *Stay ready, so you never have to get ready.*

Had I been serious about being a TV analyst, I would have prepared a reel tape before Sage Steele asked me to send her one. I should have had it done way in advance, so if I randomly got the chance to share a suite with Sage Steele, I could shoot my shot with ease. But I wasn't ready. So, instead of a layup, I was busy trying to make a half-court shot. There I was, the week after meeting her, scrambling to hire a videographer and trying to get a reel tape edited. It was just a hot mess. I missed my deadline and likely missed my opportunity, and I had no one to blame but myself. And, sadly, I didn't miss the opportunity because I didn't have the talent, or even because of fear (because I overcame that, remember?). I missed it because I wasn't ready.

It's been a couple of years since this happened, and to this day I've never sent her anything because I was too embarrassed at how unprepared I was and how late the reel tape would get to her. The takeaway here is that if you don't stay ready, you'll likely miss out on your blessing. It's like walking into an interview and someone asks for your résumé, and you have to go home to draft one. By the time you draft, edit, and send to a few friends for review, the job has been filled. You're too late—you missed your shot. There's not much worse than mustering up the courage (because it takes courage) to shoot your shot, and missing the shot because you weren't ready.

You never know who you'll randomly meet in an airport, on social media, or in a football suite. It's imperative that you're always ready for your big break, whenever it shows up.

If you want to be a model, have a comp card (a composite card with a variety of photos used like a business card) with you everywhere you go. If you're a rapper, have a handful of your mixtapes with you at all times. If you want to start your own company and are looking for investors, have a business plan saved on your computer, ready to attach to an email at a moment's notice. Get my point? You have to stay ready, so you don't end up like me and have to get ready!

If you've pinpointed your dream or goal, start working on it right now. Don't put it off. I urge you to put this book down and go work on whatever it is you've been putting off—your website, business cards, comp card, mixtape, EP, or business plan. You want to be as prepared as possible when God sends you your Sage Steele, who could be right around the corner.

AGENT YOU:
TAKE ACTION!

1. Reflect on times when fear prevented you from taking your shot.

   - Has fear ever prevented you from pursuing your dream? If so, what do you wish you'd done differently, or what can you start doing differently right now (e.g., not indulge in self-defeatist thought patterns, such as, *No one's ever going to take me seriously, so why should I even bother?*)?

- Have you ever taken your shot in spite of your fear? If so, how were you able to accomplish this? And how can you remind yourself of this victory the next time fear threatens to paralyze you? For instance, can you make a list of victories to revisit any time you feel afraid or insecure?

2. How can you stay ready, right now? In this chapter, I listed several ways you can stay ready. Make a list of three tasks you can work on today so you're prepared when opportunity comes your way. If you're unsure of what you can or should do to prepare, consult a trusted friend or mentor or ask someone who works in the industry.

Stay ready, so you
don't have to *get* ready.

CHAPTER SEVEN

Get Comfortable
with Losing

n almost any industry, a person's business is nothing without its clients or customers. What is a nail salon if no one patronizes it? Who cares if you're a fancy fashion designer if no one wears your clothes? It's no different in sports. You can only be a sports agent when you have a client (i.e., an athlete you represent). Having clients is the single most important part of being a business owner. Getting those clients is the most difficult part of my job. How do I get an athlete to sign with me? Well, that's the million-dollar question.

Recruiting. Let's start this section by saying: *It sucks!* My job as an agent is to convince a twentysomething that I am smart enough, I am organized enough and, God help me, I am cool enough to represent him in the NFL Draft. And before you can pitch your "coolness" to the player, you have to . . . wait for it . . . get him to answer the phone. My strategy can be easily analogized with an obsessed girlfriend: I'll shoot him a text telling him how great I am. If he doesn't respond, I'll call him. If that doesn't work, clearly I'm sliding into his direct messages. And as a last resort, I just show up.

Let me share the story of when I recruited my first college player. After messaging him on all social platforms, texting him, and calling him with no success, I decided I'd go to his game and introduce myself. I believed that if I could get in front of him, I could convince him I was good at my job, I cared about athletes, I'd work harder than any other agent in the business, and I'd be there when football was over.

Because I couldn't afford a plane ticket, I hopped in my car and entered his school address in my GPS. Six hours one way. That's okay, I thought. This is the price you pay for signing good athletes.

Can I throw something in this story for nothing more than pure pity? (Listen, sometimes a girl needs some pity.) I drove six hours there and then six hours back *on my birthday.*

Thank you for coming to my pity party. Now back to your regularly scheduled programming.

My emotions were all over the place. First, I was so excited. I was thinking: *Wow, here I go to recruit my first client as a full-time, registered NFL agent. I am about to change the world.* I had Beyoncé-level confidence. Then the excitement turned to nerves. I tried to calm myself by taking slow, deep breaths over and over.

I finally arrived at the game. I didn't have a ticket, so I sat in my car in the parking lot until the game ended. While waiting, I rehearsed in the mirror. "Hi, my name is Nicole Lynn. I know I am not what you were expecting, but I am one of the best sports agents you'll ever meet." Or, "Hi! No big deal, but I just drove six hours on my birthday to see you. When I say I am dedicated to your success, I mean that wholeheartedly."

When the game finally ended, I walked over to the area where friends and family wait for the players to come out. I scanned the perimeter. Nothing unexpected: easily identifiable family members and girlfriends wearing homemade jerseys with their player's number on the back; superfans hoping to get an autograph; and compliance, watching to make sure nothing fishy went down. One by one, I watched the players emerge from the locker room. As an agent or family member of a football player, you learn that some players come out quickly after a game, and others take what seems like a lifetime. Like, dude, what are you doing in there? Shower, talk to media, and get out here! Anyway, I digress.

The players started to trickle out. I'd saved the player's picture on my phone, and because football players wear helmets, it's hard to remember what they look like (and remember that I am the worst with facial recognition). *Is that him? Nope. That's totally him . . . wait, no.* In the midst of me scrutinizing the player's picture and comparing it to every person who walked out the gate, one of the worst possible things happened. It started to *rain*. And I don't mean a sprinkle—I mean full-on, pouring-down rain.

So, there I was, standing outside the gate of a college football stadium, in the rain, with no umbrella. Before you know it, I had mascara running down my face, my hair was puffing up because *black girl problems,* and to make matters worse (back to my pity party), I was wearing heels. I know you're probably thinking, *Why were you in heels?* Here's the logic behind one of the stupidest decisions I've ever made: I am only

5 feet 4.5 inches, and I'm almost always in heels. I feel more confident in heels, but even I can admit that it was ridiculous to wear heels that day.

As it rained harder, all I could think was: *God, please don't let my heels sink in the mud. Please don't let my heels sink in the mud.* Of course, my heels started sinking in the mud, and down, down I went.

And then, out came the player.

I walked over to him, with my face covered with smeared makeup, my hair a mess, and my clothes soaking wet. I thought: *Maybe this will show him I'm dedicated and clearly all in, because just about no one can convince me to stand in the rain and get my hair wet.* With as much confidence as I could muster, I stood in front of him and said: "Hi! My name is Nicole Lynn—I am a sports agent. I used to work on Wall Street, I am smart, I am a hard worker, and I would love to get to tell you more about what I can do for you in this year's draft."

<Insert long silence.>

If you could have seen the look on his face, it was like he was on an episode of *Punk'd,* that TV show where Ashton Kutcher played pranks on people. He started looking around, like he was trying to determine if cameras were hidden in the bushes and Ashton was going to jump out. He then gave me this sideways look, poked his finger toward the middle of my sternum, and asked, "*You're* a sports agent?"

I turned my head to see who else was watching. Then I said: "Yep, I am a sports agent. I know I don't look like Jerry Maguire, but we do the same thing."

The next sixty seconds are a bit of a blur, but what I do remember is him hysterically laughing and walking off. Can I tell you that I will never, ever forget the sound of this guy's laugh? It's ingrained in me for life.

I stood there in utter shock as the rain continued to drip down my face. I was so embarrassed, I rushed to my car without making eye contact with anyone. I got inside, pulled off my heels, threw the muddy shoes on the floor of the passenger seat, and slid on my flip-flops. I then did what any normal human being would have done in this situation. I busted out crying. And not just a few tears. I ugly cried.

In the middle of crying, I calmed down enough to call my friend Crystal. She answered with an excited tone, and the first thing she said was, "How did it go?"

Sobbing, I told her, "I can't do this. He just walked away from me. Like, totally just ignored me. I can't do this job. I am a black girl—no one will ever take me seriously. It was horrible. I was not made for this!" Whew—talk about self-destruction.

And then, to my surprise, my friend does the single most inappropriate thing possible: she starts to laugh. *I cannot believe this! How dare she laugh at me! Did she not hear me? He embarrassed me! He ignored me! I drove six hours* on my birthday *to see this kid and he did not give me the time of day. And now she is laughing?* I am fuming!

She eventually said a lot of nice things to try to make me feel better. Two comments stood out in my mind, and I'll never forget them. First, she said I'd remember this moment and, one day, I'd use it as a testimony when telling my story about becoming a sports agent. (Fine. She was right, dang it!) The second thing she said really resonated with me: "Nicole, you may have lost the battle today, but you didn't lose the war. If you're going to be a winner, you have to get comfortable with losing."

Such a life-changing statement: you have to get comfortable with losing.

She didn't say I *may need* to get comfortable with losing because I *might* lose, but that I *have to* get comfortable with losing because I *would* lose. Let me say that a different way: *You* have to get comfortable with losing because *you* will lose at some point. All winners lose. In fact, in the beginning, many winners lose more than they win.

If you've made it this far in the book, I hope you have some idea of your purpose in life and are now strategizing how you will fulfill that purpose. As you step onto that path, I felt I needed to prepare you for the inevitable: losing. It will happen, no matter how good you are at what you do, no matter how prepared you are, no matter how hard you work. Losing is part of the game—it is part of your journey.

After recruiting that player and losing that night in the rain, I had no clue that I'd continue losing that entire year. I recruited twenty-plus players, and each one told me no. Told me I wasn't good enough. Told me they didn't believe in me. Told me I was second best or not even in the running. And let me tell you something: there's something extremely personal and uncomfortable in being a woman whose entire career consists of begging a man for a yes and being told no, over and over.

More than anything else, losing will make you question whether you're good enough and diminish your confidence. Losing can be soul crushing. And straight-up embarrassing. Also, the more you lose, the more those around you will start to expect you to lose. "Oh, you know Bobby and his rap dream." "Susie is always starting and failing at some business." "Joey got a tryout with an NFL team, but his career is way past dead." All of a sudden, your friends and family are calling your dream and life-calling a hobby. Their words, or lack thereof, can play a huge role in your self-confidence and will to continue. The next thing you know, you're second-guessing yourself, finding yourself in a slump with a loser's mentality. People stop believing in you, and then you stop believing in yourself. It's a vicious cycle. I urge you to prepare yourself for losing, because it will happen, it will happen often, and it will not be easy.

So, how do you get comfortable with losing? You learn *how* to lose. Here are several ways you can prepare yourself for the inevitable.

BUILD A WINNER'S MENTALITY

Verbally remind yourself that you're a winner, to build up your confidence. Remind yourself of the critical losses that other successful people have had. I like to recite them when stuff hits the fan: "Remember, Nicole—Walt Disney was fired from the *Kansas City Star* because his editor felt he lacked imagination and had no good ideas. Oprah Winfrey lost her first TV job because the producer said she was unfit for TV.[1] Look at where they ended up!"

What is a winner's mentality? Winners accept losing and keep losing until they win. Losers give up when they lose. That's the difference. Having a winner's mentality is as simple as that: a winner has the grit to continually push through the losses. Unfortunately, not everyone is built to overcome adversity. But you can be, if you choose to be. Say it now, and say it as often as you need: "I am a winner, no matter how much I lose."

NEVER GET TOO HIGH, NEVER GET TOO LOW

Have you ever been fired twice in one week? By the same client? I have. Yep, you're hearing that right. Some insane football player fired the best agent on the planet—*me*. (Kidding, sort of.) It was five years into my career, and I'd never been fired by an active player. When you're a sports agent, you *will* get fired. More than three hundred players per year fire their agents, and I'd been lucky enough to escape that fate for years. Then the grim reaper caught up to me, and I was fired. There was nothing I could have done differently, and I did nothing wrong. Sometimes your losses are genuinely no fault of your own.

Being fired by a player I considered as close as family devastated me. In the past, I would've been anxious and depressed. I would've spent a lot of time beating myself up, trying to determine what I could have done to prevent it, and why I wasn't good enough. But this time was different. I told myself, *Instead of letting my emotions control me and control this situation, I am going to choose the emotions I want to feel, because I am in control.* I allowed myself a moment to be disappointed, then immediately started saying repeatedly: "I am going to be all right. This is part of the industry and part of the journey. It will not steal my joy." I used this opportunity to practice controlling my emotions when at my lowest point.

Being a sports agent comes with a lot of highs and even more lows. Finding balance and reining in my emotions is one of the hardest parts of my job. There's not many things worse than a player firing you, and feeling like you've experienced a bad breakup. There's also not many things sweeter than signing a first-round draft pick. I navigate the emotional roller coaster of this agent life by never allowing myself to get too high or too low in any situation. When you're the agent of your own life, you must mentally prepare for the wins and the losses. You have to decide which emotion, and the amount of that emotion, you'll give to a situation, instead of the emotion choosing for you.

OVERCOME FEAR

Fear takes many forms—fear of embarrassment, fear of failure, fear of making a wrong turn. Did you know that most people will never win, not because they keep losing, but because their fear of losing prevents them from ever starting? How can we overcome fear? One tactic is to not live your life chasing hypotheticals. I hate hypotheticals, which lead you down the "what if" rabbit trail. *What if no one comes to my event? What if no one watches my YouTube channel? What if they hate my cooking?* This is a dangerous place to be, a place where fear is watered and grows.

When you find yourself chasing the hypothetical, start asking yourself the opposite: What if the best-case scenario happened? I use this a lot on planes because I hate flying. My initial thoughts used to be: *What if the plane crashes? What if there are three hours of turbulence, and I have an anxiety attack?* Instead my mindset should be: *What if there isn't one bump the entire trip? What if it's so smooth I'm able to get work done? What if I can catch up on sleep too?*

Change every hypothetical to a positive, and it will alter your mindset and your life.

FAIL FORWARD

Since we know failures will happen on this journey to purposeful lives and careers, we should use those failures as teachable moments. How can we better ourselves? The next time something doesn't go as planned, ask yourself how you could have done something differently. Sometimes there was nothing you could have done differently, like when I got fired by a client though I did nothing wrong. Regardless, that situation was still a teachable moment. During that failure, I was able to practice controlling my emotions. Now, the next time it happens (God forbid), I'm less likely to be a nervous wreck.

Think of having a toolbox full of skills that you've accumulated over the course of your life. Every time you have a failure or loss, add to the toolbox. For example, did you launch a new location for your business, and no one showed up? Add different marketing strategies to your toolbox. Learn them in and out. Did a customer leave your company a bad review on a website? Brainstorm ways to improve your customers' experience, and add those to your toolbox. Take the time to write them down. You'll be surprised at how much you learn from all your different experiences, especially when you're intentional about documenting this information.

HAVE YOUR PITY PARTY,
THEN GET THE HECK UP!

When you lose, it's okay to be disappointed, sad, or discouraged. Emotions are supposed to be felt but can become problematic when they cause you to act negatively. In other words, you can be discouraged, but don't allow the sadness to make you give up. You can be sad, but don't get so sad you need to take two weeks off to recover. Emotions are only an issue when the emotions control you, versus you controlling the emotions.

Create a practical plan for how you'll deal with losing, so you don't stay down long. Maybe you have a specific friend you call to encourage you. Maybe you take the evening off from work, to refresh and reset. Maybe you get a mani-pedi. We all sometimes need pick-me-ups, but they're harder to bring to mind in a moment of distress. Have a list ready!

COUNT ALL YOUR WINS

When you've experienced many losses and been told no many times, it can be hard to find the positive. But I promise you, it's there! We must count the wins we *do* have, even when they seem small. Remember, going for it in the first place is a win. Give yourself credit.

How long did you think about trying something new, changing careers, opening a business, or making a cold call? So much anxiety, preparation, and back-and-forth before you made the jump. Who cares if you failed on the first try? You took the risk, and that in itself is a win. Maybe you haven't sold a single item from your new pop-up shop, but you did upload all the photos on the new website, something you've dreaded doing for months. You uploaded them—that's a win! You finally got the courage to send out your résumé, and you've gotten nothing but rejection letters. But you sent the résumés—that's a win.

We have many wins along the way, which often are overshadowed by the losses. I encourage you not to lose sight of those wins. Every time you fail, sit down and make a list of at least three wins that also happened.

NEVER LOSE SIGHT OF THE ULTIMATE GOAL

Although I always have my ultimate goal in mind, I like to break it up into smaller goals along the way. But sometimes when one of our micro goals doesn't work out, we get tripped up and forget that it's just one hurdle in the race. The thought of the ultimate goal, the finish line, should fuel your fire. Focusing on the loss of one battle when there's an entire war to be won will take you off track. Wars are won over time, battle by battle, just as football games are won over four quarters. One quarter doesn't win or lose a game, and one loss in your journey doesn't dictate if you'll finish the race.

I now represent over twenty-five clients, including football players, coaches, softball players, ESPY-nominated athletes, and even rappers. But when I look back on my career, for every client who told me yes, twenty told me no. For every time I won, I lost ten times prior. During this journey, I never took my eyes off of the ultimate goal.

I truly believe part of the reason I'm successful is because I've gotten comfortable with losing. And losing isn't always bad. It can make your story that much sweeter: "I had fifty athletes tell me no before one said yes," or "I had ten investors turn down my pitch and now I own a multimillion-dollar company," or "Columbia Records told me that there wasn't a hit on the album, but the album went quadruple platinum" (the latter is Beyoncé's story).[2]

Get comfortable with losing, and watch your life change.

AGENT YOU:
TAKE ACTION!

1. Use affirmations to focus, stay positive, and keep your emotions in check. Mentally prepare yourself for failure, so you're not derailed when it happens.

   - If you know and admire someone successful, research that person's backstory. Did he or she experience losses before winning? If so, how were those challenges navigated? How can you use that story to keep you motivated?
   - Transform your "what if" worst-case scenarios to "what if" best-case scenarios. For instance, instead of saying, "What if no one attends my grand-opening event?" say, "What if so many people attend my grand-opening event that it's

standing room only, and the line wraps around
the block?"

- Make a list of at least three positive outlets for
the emotions you experience when you lose,
then remind yourself of them. For example, "If
I get turned down for the promotion, I will treat
myself to a spa day, then ask my supervisor what
I can do to put myself in a better position for
the next promotion."

2. When you lose, consider that an opportunity to
add skills to your toolbox. What did you learn
from the experience that can set you up for
success next time?

3. Count all your wins. It's easy to allow
disappointment to cloud our vision instead of
acknowledging even the small victories. In what
ways, small or big, did you win on your journey,
even if a particular effort didn't succeed? Write
down at least three things you can celebrate
as wins.

You will lose, but you
win when you keep going.

CHAPTER EIGHT

Do All You Can,
Then Do No More

The year 2018 was the busiest of my life. Let me paint the picture:

I'd just signed the young female rapper That Girl Lay Lay as a client, and we hit the ground running. In what seemed like back-to-back weeks, we were shooting commercials for Mitsubishi and appearing on *The Ellen DeGeneres Show*. Meanwhile, I was preparing witnesses and exhibits for a multimillion-dollar trial. Oh, and it was football season. So, in the middle of preparing witness outlines for trial, I was hopping on a plane twice a week to see a client.

Amid everything else going on, I was supposed to be recruiting new players for the next draft, but I had no time. I couldn't sleep at night because I knew I was behind on recruiting, to a point that was beyond recovery. I had to start preparing myself for the inevitable: I wouldn't have a client to represent in the 2019 NFL Draft.

One day, while sitting in my office, I got a text message from another agent in my agency, Ken, who asked: "How is recruiting going? What college guys have you met with?" My heart sunk. I looked at the calendar and realized it was somehow the end of November, and I had done little to no recruiting, besides two meetings over the summer. At that point, it was way too late to try to recruit players. I could possibly score last-minute meetings with a couple college players, but that was unlikely, and even if I did manage to get them to agree to meet with me, I had no time to do so. My law job was burying me, and my current list of clients kept me busy and on the road.

During my freak-out, in my spirit I felt God say I had done all I could, and he'd meet me halfway. I called my husband and confidently said, "I've decided I'm giving my recruiting to God." I felt so strongly that God was telling me it was time for me to rest in him and believe he would meet me right where I was.

Over the next month, I didn't recruit. In fact, I didn't recruit the rest of the year. I decided to believe that God would bring the recruits to me.

This is a crazy way to think in my industry. In no world do recruits come to *you*.

Period.

In all actuality, you come to them, and they run away. Even so, I can't explain the strong sense of peace I had after feeling God's message in my spirit.

I remember one of my close friends telling me, "It's the busiest season of your life, and even if you wanted to do more in recruiting, you could not."

Let me take a minute to dive into this thought: *Even if you wanted to do more, you could not.* In this book, I talk a lot about working toward your goals, and doing so every single day. As you're reading this book, you probably realize I have a non-stop personality. My friends remind me that the way I work is the exception and not the rule. That the majority of people aren't built like me and don't think the way I do. But if you find that your personality is similar to mine, or you simply find yourself unable to do anything else in working toward a goal, take this advice: Sometimes you have to do all you can, then do no more. When you have given all you can to something, there comes a time when you have to give it to God.

The Bible says, "Faith without deeds is dead" (James 2:26). For many years, I misconstrued this scripture. I focused and relied solely on the "deeds" portion of this scripture and tended to forget about the other, most important part: faith. This scripture tells us that we can only do so much alone. In other words, our works can be great, but they are done in vain if we don't factor God into the equation.

When I decided to give my recruiting to God, it was me trusting him and telling him he has control of my life, and I had done all that was *humanly* possible. If God can heal the sick and raise the dead, why couldn't he bring recruits to me? *Show out, God!*

● ● ●

So, there I was, going about my life as football season ended. I began to see other agents announcing their big draft signings on social media, when I randomly got a call that Quinnen Williams wanted to meet with me. First of all, who was Quinnen Williams? I quickly researched and discovered that Quinnen was the number one player in college football. I thought: *Is this a practical joke? Why in the world would a possibly number one overall pick want to meet with me? Excuse me, but I am a peasant.* (I was experiencing imposter syndrome to the max.)

When I finally realized I wasn't being punked, I learned that I had less than a day to prepare for the biggest meeting of my life. I wasted no time and stayed up all night working with our team on a presentation we hoped would knock his socks off. I jumped on a plane and within forty-eight hours of that first call, I stood in front of Quinnen Williams and his family. *Someone slap me—am I dreaming?*

As I began, I decided to be transparent from the outset. Of course, I believe I'm the best agent for Quinnen, because I believe I am one of the most dedicated and hardest-working agents in the business. There is no question in my mind that I'd kill for Quinnen. But the truth was that I'd never represented a first-round draft pick before, and Quinnen was a first-round lock. No matter how amazing my personality or how much my work ethic shined through, I couldn't hide the hard truth: I was young, new, and inexperienced.

I started my presentation and could barely catch my breath, because I was talking so fast. I still remember Quinnen sitting there, arms crossed across his chest and little expression on his face. He didn't ask a single question. After it was all over, I stood there looking around the room, waiting for some type of approval, but Quinnen was silent. Other family members started to talk and ask questions, so I began to answer. A few minutes later, Quinnen chimed in out of nowhere: "I have a question."

I looked up, smiled, and said, "Sure, anything."

He then said, "I don't understand how you don't have any first-rounders yet . . . because you're a beast!"

I fainted.

Okay, not really, but I fainted in my head.

I later found out that Q was choosing me as his agent.

Shameless plug for my sports agency: It was an agency effort. Although I'm grateful to represent Quinnen, I wasn't solely responsible for securing him as a client. Our entire team played a role. We have the best marketing people, operations people, and agents in the business. We are all-hands-on-deck for a player of his caliber, and I couldn't have succeeded alone.

After I found out Q had chosen me as his agent, we immediately started preparing him for the draft. During one of our car rides, he asked if I wanted to know why he'd chosen me, out of all the agents he'd met with.

"Yes, of course I do!" I said.

He told me he'd chosen me for two reasons. First, he recognized that I'd never had a first-rounder. He wanted to help me just as much as I would help him. He realized that if he went number one overall, that would be great, but a lot of players had gone number one overall. But what if he went number one overall while also making history, while also effecting change, while also assisting women in their journey to have a true presence in sports?

I could barely believe a twenty-year-old had thought through his decision like that, with such a mature and selfless way of thinking.

His second reason for picking me was even more interesting. A few years back, I'd won an award presented by The Hustle and Salesforce, called "2X Woman of the Year." I was asked to speak at an event honoring the award recipients. I talked about recruiting my first player, and how I drove six hours to meet him, stood in the rain, and he dissed me.

(Remember that story in chapter 7?) I have no idea how Quinnen found that speech, but he did.

He said: "I watched your speech and saw how the player dissed you, but you still didn't give up. That is when I decided that I wanted an agent that would go that hard for me every single day."

You can't tell me that wasn't God. What I considered the lowest moment of my career turned into one of the reasons I signed my first first-rounder. And as I sat there, I was reminded of these words: *Do all you can, then do no more.* God told me he'd meet me halfway, and he truly showed up in a major way. Sometimes, you must let go and let God. No matter the amount of work you do toward walking in your purpose and being successful in that purpose, you will never reach your full potential if you don't bring God into the equation.

And by no means am I saying, "Oh, hey—sit back and relax, and God will bring you all your hopes and dreams, and you don't have to do anything." What I am saying is that God will meet you right where you are. I still put in the work and was prepared, but I got to a point where I had to let go and let God. I gave all I could, and I gave my very, very best.

So, listen here: You have worked, you have prayed, you have been diligent. And now, it's time to give the rest to God and watch him rock your world!

EVEN IF HE DOESN'T

In writing this chapter, I feel it's important to prepare you for the alternative. Just because you let go and let God doesn't mean you'll suddenly have everything you've ever prayed for or at the time you specifically asked for it. I don't want my story of God showing up with a first-round NFL Draft pick to give you a false sense of reality. That year could have easily gone the other way, and I could have signed no players.

What happens when God doesn't answer our prayers as we think he should? Or doesn't do it on our desired timeline?

Meet Taylor Moore: attorney by day, wife, podcaster, life coach, and women's spiritual leader by night. I met Taylor while working at my law firm and was immediately enamored by her love for people and her true faith in God. Taylor is the epitome of "let go and let God."

Taylor and her husband had been trying to get pregnant for two years. Have you ever met someone and just knew she was meant to be a mom? I mean this in the most respectful and complimentary way: Taylor is one of those women. She has supermom written all over her. (You read her bio above, right?)

I was privy to Taylor's pregnancy journey and was believing and praying that God would bless her with a child. One night, Taylor came to my house for our weekly TV night (*Little Fires Everywhere*—can we say "best show ever"?). While hanging out, she updated me that, unfortunately, she still wasn't pregnant. When you're friends with someone who's trying to get pregnant, you join her on the emotional roller coaster. At that point, I was fully invested in Taylor's journey and felt crushed when the news was anything but positive.

Taylor then told me she felt God was pushing her to publicly share her journey of trying to get pregnant. As many of you are aware, thousands of women struggle to conceive, and Taylor felt committed to sharing her story to encourage other women and couples walking the same path. I knew this wasn't an easy decision for Taylor because she had no idea what the outcome would be. Think about it: usually we get the testimony from someone after receiving the blessing. It's less common for someone to be so vulnerable and transparent and take us along on the journey through the storm.

Taylor's words to me were: "It's hard, because I don't know what is going to happen. I can pray for a child, but I have no idea what God's will is for me in this situation. But I still believe I have to share this, and whatever God has for me in whatever timing, I will be grateful."

When Taylor said this, the first thought that came to mind for me was the story of the fiery furnace, in the Book of Daniel in the Bible. This well-known story relates to faith and trusting in God. It takes place when King Nebuchadnezzar was the ruler of the Babylonian empire. He had a golden statue built and ordered all the people to worship the statue. Anyone who didn't would be thrown into a furnace and burned alive. During this time, it was common for kings to build statues for the people to worship.

Three Hebrew young men, Shadrach, Meshach, and Abednego, refused to worship the king's idol because they worshipped the one true living God. They told the king they had no desire or intention to worship the golden statue, which infuriated the king. The young men told him: "King Nebuchadnezzar, we do not need to defend ourselves before you in this matter. If we are thrown into the blazing furnace, the God we serve is able to deliver us from it, and he will deliver us from Your Majesty's hand. But even if he does not, we want you to know, Your Majesty, that we will not serve your gods or worship the image of gold you have set up" (Daniel 3:16–18).

"But even if he does not."

Wow! That level of faith and commitment is almost unfathomable. If God didn't save me from a furnace, especially if I were being tossed in because of love and loyalty to him, I'm going to be at least a tiny bit mad. (As we can see, God is still working on me.) As the story goes, Shadrach, Meshach, and Abednego are thrown into the furnace, but God, in his almighty power, delivers them while they're *in* the fire. Not before, but *in*. Even on their way to the furnace, they never once questioned that God had the ability to save them. And their faith in knowing that God's plan was best was shown through their belief that, even if he didn't save them, their faith in God wouldn't waver.

What happens when God doesn't show up for us on the timeline we expect or in the manner we think he should? Taylor took a risk. She had her own timeline when she wanted a child, but she decided to surrender her desires to God and trust his timing and his will. She said, in effect, I believe God will give me a child, but even if he doesn't do it in the way I expect, I'm still going to honor and worship him. She made a decision to trust God's plan for her life over her own.

To truly let go and let God, you have to be comfortable with letting God do whatever is in his will. In other words, letting go of how you want the situation to play out and letting God step in to orchestrate the situation in his perfect will. Letting go and letting God means being okay with the outcome God has decided for you and being okay with his timing. It's walking in the fiery furnace and believing: My God will save me, *but even if he doesn't,* I'll still worship him. It's saying:

- I'm believing God for the job, but even if he doesn't, I'll still honor and worship him.
- I'm believing God for healing, but even if he doesn't, I'll still honor and worship him.

- I'm believing God will fix my marriage, but even if he doesn't, I'll still honor and worship him.
- I'm believing God will bring my kids home, but even if he doesn't, I'll still honor and worship him.

That is how you let go and let God.

HOW TO LET GO AND LET GOD

Realize that what is for you *is for you.*

In giving God control of your life and truly letting go, you are letting go of the notion that you know what's best for your life. We can't say we trust and believe in God, but then tell God we don't like his plan for us. We have to trust that he knows what's best and that what is meant for us won't pass us by. God is your Creator and knows you better than any person on Earth. He has a perfect plan for your life that may not always look like what you've imagined. Letting go is giving God control and having faith that you'll receive the *best* outcome—not necessarily *your* outcome. Remember, your story is already written. Whatever is meant for you is for you, and God's timing is always best.

I can't thank God enough for the times he has answered my prayers with a no. Think about some of the prayers you've prayed over your lifetime. Can you point to any prayers where God didn't give you exactly what you wanted? Can you point to some where you're now grateful he didn't do exactly what you asked? Think about that boyfriend you prayed so desperately to stay with, but it didn't work out. Now, looking back, you think, *Whew, I dodged a bullet!*

As humans, our wants can blind us. Remember that God knows the desires of your heart, but he also has a view of the bigger picture. We only see one chapter of our lives at a time, whereas God knows the end of the story. So, I thank God for the times he answered some of my prayers with a no. Thank you, God, for not saying yes to my prayer to get into Duke, because then I wouldn't have met my husband. Thank you, God, for not saying yes and letting me marry little Johnny, my ten-year-old crush. Thank you, God, for not saying yes and giving me that sales job, because I never would have found my purpose. In the moment, I didn't understand, but God knew exactly what I needed.

GIVE GOD YOUR WORRIES

I hate to fly. Part of the reason I hate flying is because I am a control freak. I like to be in control of situations, and being on an airplane is the least control I can have in almost anything. When I board a plane, I pray that God gives me traveling mercies and a safe trip. Sitting there in my seat, I have no choice but to give it to God that I'll arrive safely. However, I'm not truly letting go and letting God if I'm worrying the entire flight. Truly giving it to God is making a conscious decision to let go of the worry and believe that, whatever the outcome, it's in our best interests. So, when you're finally able to give up control, do so with the intention of also placing your worries in God's hands. The Bible says, "Cast your cares on the Lord and he will sustain you; he will never let the righteous be shaken" (Psalm 55:22).

I truly believe my career wouldn't be where it is had I not given my recruiting worries to God that day. When I was insufficient in my own might, God met me there and brought me my biggest recruit at that time, in the most unexpected and unconventional way.

Oh, yeah, and Taylor got pregnant the very next month, after she surrendered her desires to the Lord. She and her husband now have a sweet baby girl (her name is Faith—how fitting!).

All this is to say, whatever it is about your life that you're desperately trying to hold on to, let go and let God. Watch and see what he will do.

AGENT YOU: TAKE ACTION!

1. Think about this idea: "Even if you wanted to do more, you could not."

   - Are there any areas of your life where you simply cannot do more? Perhaps you've put in an insane number of hours at work, sacrificing your relationships and health, yet still haven't made partner. Or maybe you've tried everything you can think of to salvage a relationship, yet no improvement is being made.
   - Write down at least one area in your life that you have done all you could and need to let go and let God.

2. Consider an area or areas in your life where you're already trusting God, regardless of the outcome.

   - One way to further commit to trusting him in that situation is to complete the following sentence: "I'm believing God for _____, but even if he doesn't, I'll still honor and worship him."

3. Another way to trust God with the outcome is to reflect on times when his answer to your prayer was no.

   - List at least three times in your life you're grateful that God said no instead of yes.
   - How do those situations help you appreciate God's plan for your life?

When you let go and let God, you also trust him with the outcome.

CHAPTER NINE

Ditch Imposter Syndrome

I t was April 26, 2019, and I walked into the greenroom of the NFL Draft to join my client Quinnen Williams, the top player in college football. The minute I entered the room, the goose bumps began, and I could barely catch my breath. I wanted to remember every detail about this night. I inhaled deeply and smelled a mixture of cologne and fresh air. I scanned the room and noticed the stage, the fans lining up in the streets, the signs, the camera crews, and the other draft picks entering the room, along with their agents and family members. And I felt my own heartbeat racing a hundred miles per hour.

The NFL Draft greenroom is reserved for the top twenty-five players in the country, their families, and their respective agents. Top prospects sit and wait for the moment they have worked for their entire lives: their name to be called by Roger Goodell, stating that they have been drafted into the National Football League. And sitting right next to the NFL Draft hopeful is a person he trusts and has chosen to help navigate his football career—his agent.

As I looked around, I expected someone would kindly ask me to leave, assuming this little black girl must have snuck in. Or someone would ask me which draft pick is my boyfriend. Or someone would hand me their empty plate or ask for directions to the bathroom.

We entered our section, which had lounge-style couches in a *U* shape. In the middle of the section was a chair next to a telephone, which was obviously for the draft pick. Quinnen took his seat. His family sat on the couches, and I watched and waited to see which seat remained open for me.

As I stood there, a peer agent walked up and tapped my shoulder. He gently said: "Hey, that chair right next to your guy—it's for the agent. It's for you."

For me? I thought. I tried not to look too surprised, thanked him for the direction, and sat next to my client, waiting for the draft to begin.

The minute I sat, with cameras surrounding us, I immediately regretted my outfit. Choosing an outfit for the NFL Draft had been an event in itself. What do you wear to the Draft when you're an agent who also happens to be a woman? I remember googling "NFL Draft woman agent" over and over, and found nothing. I asked female reporters, and they weren't much help either. I decided on a fitted, long-sleeve black dress with silver rhinestones perfectly placed throughout, complemented by a black, red-bottom, closed-toe heel. I feared that fans would assume I was my client's girlfriend or wife, and I started to beat myself up for not wearing a suit. *How stupid could you be, Nicole? This isn't the Grammys! You should have worn a suit. Rookie mistake.*

As I wallowed in my sorrows about my outfit choice, a couple of the biggest agents in the game walked up to congratulate me for the incredible moment that was about to take place: making history as the first black woman with an NFL Draft pick that high. However, it didn't matter what they said. I still had this gut-wrenching feeling like I wasn't supposed to be there.

I've heard over and over again that women must "get a seat at the table." I, too, teach this concept and urge women to get a seat at the table early. There I was, in the greenroom, with a literal seat at the draft table, and I still couldn't help feeling like I didn't belong.

I was not only the only female NFL agent in the greenroom but also the youngest NFL agent in the room, both in age and agent experience. Some of those agents had worked for decades to be worthy of sitting in that greenroom. Other agents had been in the greenroom year after year and were comfortable in the greenroom.

And then there's me, I thought. *The imposter.*

The time had come: the NFL Draft was about to begin. The first pick went exactly as expected—Kyler Murray to the Arizona Cardinals. The San Francisco 49ers had the second pick and were on the clock. The night before, I'd told Quinnen that I didn't think he'd be drafted number one or number two. He didn't want to hear that, but it was the truth, and I felt it was important to be honest. So, when the 49ers were on the clock and chose Nick Bosa, I leaned over to my client and reminded him: "We discussed this. No surprises—we were prepared for this."

He agreed. "Okay, sis."

I told myself: *You did it—you made it through the first two picks, and they went exactly as planned. You haven't failed . . . yet.* I had mentally prepared myself for the first two picks, but what I wasn't prepared for was what could happen starting at pick three. Numerous scenarios could make this draft a nightmare for me. Teams could trade up and grab a quarterback, or a team could draft an offensive player out of nowhere—it could get crazy. I'd reviewed worst-case scenarios and concluded there was a world where my client, the best player in the draft, could drop nine slots based on how teams decided to move. I prayed, *God, please just let him go three.*

The New York Jets had the number three pick, and the draft clock was reset to ten minutes. My stomach dropped. When a player is selected in the NFL Draft, the team that selects him will call prior to the pick being announced on live TV. I looked up at the draft clock. Eight minutes of the allotted ten minutes had passed, and no call. My eyes darted from my client, to the phone, and then to the camera positioned directly in front of us. I thought: *This is the moment I'll be exposed. I'm an imposter—I'm not supposed to be here. The phone won't ring, he'll fall in the draft, and everyone will see that I'm a fraud. I have failed before I even got started.*

Just as I lowered my head, trying to hold back tears (a scene captured by many photographers and that has since gone viral), the phone rang.

Quinnen picked up the phone.

"Quinnen Williams, this is Mike Maccagnan, general manager of the New York Jets. Are you ready to be a Jet?"

"Yes, sir, I am," Quinnen said, smiling. He turned to me and grabbed my shoulder to comfort me, since I'd been crying for two minutes straight. He whispered, "We did it." Those words are forever plastered in my mind. We did it. *We did it!*

In that moment I was reminded that, although in the past hour I had lost all confidence in myself and my abilities, the people surrounding me, especially my client, had never stopped believing in me. I was the only one who questioned myself.

When he hung up the phone, I jumped up and screamed, "We are going to the New York Jets, y'all." My smile never left my face that night, and I reverted to normal, reminding myself that I am the ish! *<Insert Lizzo "Truth Hurts" lyrics.>*

Before walking into that greenroom, I had believed in myself. I knew I had given my all to my client. I had advocated for my client to NFL teams. I had prepared my client for interviews, the NFL Combine, and NFL workouts. I had diligently and fervently hustled for my client, and I had every right to be in that room. But when I finally made it in the room (or "a seat at the table"), imposter syndrome set in.

Imposter syndrome is a psychological term referring to a pattern of behavior where people doubt their accomplishments and have a persistent, often internalized fear of being exposed as a fraud.[1]

Imposter syndrome is more common than you think. The cycle typically looks something like this: You have a dream, you believe in yourself, you work your butt off to accomplish that dream. Every step of the way, you know you were called for this, you are motivated and believe that no one could do it better. After more hard work than you could have ever imagined, you finally make it to "the table." You pull out the chair for your "seat at the table" you've always dreamed of. But the minute you sit down, you feel unworthy.

This vicious cycle sucks. Let's say this straight up: *It sucks!* Because at the end of the day, it's not that other people think I'm not good enough—it's just me. Me, in my own head, going nuts.

And if you're a woman or a minority, or both, you might be one of the few people—or the only person—who looks like you at your "table." Such people are the exceptions to every rule, unusual and uncommon. We crawl, kick, cry, and plead to get to the table. We fight for a seat longer and harder than our peers, and when we arrive there, we believe we aren't good enough to be there.

Can you relate?

You know what I find so interesting about my time at the NFL Draft? Although I felt like an imposter, that feeling immediately subsided when the phone rang. Why? Because the phone call symbolized public acknowledgment that I had done a good job, and my client had been drafted. But why did I need public confirmation to feel worthy? In a perfect world, in that moment I would have reminded myself why I deserved to be there, and never looked back. I would have known, even if the phone never rang, that I am still worthy.

Are you waiting for the phone to ring to feel like you are worthy? Waiting on a boss to tell you did well on an assignment to know you are a valued employee? Waiting on other moms to compliment your parenting skills to feel like a great mom? Waiting on a friend to notice your new haircut and say it looks good on you? Waiting on some guy to tell you you're beautiful before you believe it—or to tell you he loves you, so you can feel loved? (Sis, don't even get me started on this topic. We'll save it for the next book because, Lord knows, I do not have the time.) Are you sitting at "the table" right now and feeling like an imposter?

Consider this a friendly reminder: You don't need that phone call, that boss, that mom, that friend, that guy, to tell you you're worthy, you're good enough, you're beautiful. *You are!* You are already worthy. You are already good enough. I want you to tell yourself this every single day: I am *already* worthy. Go get a dry-erase marker and write those words on your mirror, or jot them on sticky notes and post where you can see them throughout the day.

More than anything, I want us to overcome imposter syndrome. How do we do this? Here are a few ideas.

CHECK YOUR TRIBE

As I sat in the greenroom, I imagined that other people saw me as I saw myself. A little black girl from the 'hood who grew up poor. A little black girl who was an intruder in a space where she didn't belong. A little black girl who was unqualified for the position and undeserving of any recognition.

Though I tried to avoid checking my phone during the draft, I briefly looked down and saw my group chat filled with many positive messages: "We're so proud of you!" "You are killing it!" How could I not feel like a boss?

Surround yourself with people who believe in you even when you don't believe in yourself. In other words, check your tribe, sis. You should have people who are constantly building you up when you need it, and even when you don't. I think your tribe is so crucial to your success that I wrote a whole chapter about it (chapter 13).

It's even more important to make sure the members of your tribe are extremely honest with you. That way, when they say you belong somewhere, you believe them—because they're also the friends who will tell you the truth even when it hurts. Create an environment where your friends are comfortable telling you the truth, so when you do receive good feedback from them, you can take it seriously, because it's more valuable. You can do this by not getting defensive when your friends provide honest, constructive criticism. Having a strong, encouraging support system is essential when those inevitable thoughts of imposter syndrome creep in and you're doing everything in your power to keep them out.

You don't have to do it alone—*ask for and receive support.*

BE OVERPREPARED

Although I struggled to believe I was worthy of "a seat at the table," I never once thought, *I wish I had done more.* I knew I'd done every single thing necessary to prepare for having a top three NFL Draft pick. I walked into that greenroom totally prepared, without a single regret. Whether I succeeded or failed on draft night, I never wanted to second-guess how I could have done something better.

Likewise, I want you to outwork the competition. If you believe a project takes three hours of preparation, take five. If you're presenting on company financials for the previous two years, learn the previous four years. When your company schedules a meeting to discuss new product ideas and asks you to come with a pitch, come with three! Be so over-prepared that you would be embarrassed for anyone to know how much time and energy you invested in the task.

When you finally get to the table, you'll find both comfort and confidence in being overprepared. You never want to be sitting at the table and questioning whether you could have done more to prepare for the role. Or whether you could have worked harder on the presentation. Or whether you could have studied more for the exam. Leave it all on the table, with no regrets.

In spite of any insecurities I had, I always promised myself that no one would ever catch me off guard. If I score a meeting with a wide receiver, I'm going to scrutinize every major wide receiver free agent deal from the past five years. The more prepared you are for your moment at the table, the less you will feel like an imposter. By that point, the truth is that you aren't an imposter—you're the real deal.

COMPARE YOURSELF TO OTHERS

When I sat in the greenroom and thought about the other agents in that room with me, it made me a little sick to my stomach. For starters, their experience tripled mine. But then I remembered that each and every one of them had experienced a first time in the greenroom. I imagined them on their first day, versus me on my first day. And in comparing the two equivalents (apples to apples), I felt better, because I knew I was just as prepared for my first time in the greenroom as they were for their first time.

Comparison is the thief of joy, they say. Although I agree with this statement in any other situation, I think comparison can help you overcome imposter syndrome. For instance, if you're at the table with your peers or with people who have similar experience levels (but perhaps look different than you), comparing yourself against them can bolster your confidence. Consider this example: *Bobby and I are both at the table, we both have three years of experience at the company, we both went to top colleges, and we both graduated with honors. We are equals. Thus, I am not an imposter.*

However, remember to compare apples to apples, not apples to oranges, because the latter is unfair to you. Don't compare your first day with someone else's hundredth day. That will indeed steal your joy. Instead, look at your peers, people with the same work experience or same education level, and realize you're just as good and at the table for a reason.

BE CONFIDENT IN WHO YOU ARE

I'm a woman in a space—at a table, if you will—seemingly created for men. A male agent gets to continue being exactly who he is, because the job was created with him in mind. It was not created for me.

The chairs at the table weren't made for me to sit in, yet I didn't try to squeeze in and make it work. I will never be "one of the guys," and as soon as I realized that and became comfortable in my own skin, my life changed forever. I brought my own chair to the table, creating a made-just-for-me seat in the male-dominated sports world.

I don't wear tennis shoes and ball caps to "fit in." You're more likely to catch me in five-inch heels, beachy waves, and a nude lipstick. A lot of sports deals are made over drinks, but I always offer coffee because I don't drink alcohol. (I don't compromise on this.) I post a lot on social media, even though my peer agents don't. I am me.

When you attempt to be someone you aren't, that is a major source of imposter syndrome. However, you can't be an imposter when you're being true to yourself. You will kick imposter syndrome's butt when you become confident in exactly who you are.

Trying to conform your looks, actions, and speech to those around you causes mental and emotional exhaustion. You'll find yourself constantly striving to maintain a façade that goes against the very nature of who you are. Not only will you be dead tired when you get home every evening and remove that day's "mask," but your work quality may start to slip too. And, sis, this is where we must draw the line. We should be utilizing that energy to perfect our craft and be the best at what we do.

How can we ever break the glass ceiling by trying to fit in, when we were made to stand out?

When you're unapologetically comfortable in your own skin, you may still feel like an imposter sometimes, just as I did in that NFL Draft greenroom. But when imposter syndrome tries to sneak in and undermine you, you'll have the necessary tools to overcome this enemy.

AGENT YOU:
TAKE ACTION!

1. Check your tribe. Surround yourself with people who believe in you even when you don't believe in yourself.

   - Who is the one person you can always count on to cheer you on but also tell it to you straight?
   - Who are the five people who consistently call/text/email you supportive and encouraging words?
   - Who, after spending time with them, fills you up and makes you feel ready to take on the world?

2. Don't just be prepared—be overprepared. Leave nothing on the table, and always be ready and willing to go above and beyond.

   - What do you know you could be doing more of, more often, to overprepare? Make a list of three ways you can overprepare for a current project.

3. Compare yourself to others. However, make sure you compare yourself to your peers, not those who are further down the path than you.

   - Who has a similar education/experience level to you?
   - If you have peers ahead of you on the path, what must you do to catch up to them?

When you're true
to yourself, you'll
become more confident
and overcome
imposter syndrome.

CHAPTER TEN

Score a Seat at the Table

No matter what industry you work in, if they do not give you a seat at the table, feel free to make your own table. But even more important, get to whatever table fast. (The information and tips I share in this chapter can apply to anyone who's ever been marginalized in their career, but I'm especially speaking to all the women out there.)

I think it's important to acknowledge that you can find purpose in your current nine-to-five job. For many people, your passion is what you're already doing. You may be reading this book and saying: "Look, sis—I like what I'm doing, but I wish I could move up the food chain. I've been in the same role and feel I deserve something better." Let's talk about how to live your best life and be the agent of your own career, when your current nine-to-five is your passion.

In one study of 317 companies, women make up only 21 percent of C-suite executives and hold only 28 percent of senior vice president positions.[1] I can't help but wonder why women aren't given the leadership positions they deserve. Why are they consistently overlooked for partnerships or C-suite executive positions? Why are women treated differently than their male counterparts?

Most of us have heard the TED Talks and the motivational speeches about women getting a seat at the table. And most of us have heard that if a seat isn't available, create your own table. Although I agree with both schools of thought, I believe there needs to be more emphasis not only on women getting a seat at the table but getting that seat *early* in their career. In fact, I believe this is the number one key to a woman's success in corporate America.

The disparate treatment between men and women in the workplace doesn't start when both a woman and man are finally up for a board-level position or being considered for CEO; it starts when both individuals are at the bottom and in their respective entry-level positions. Unfortunately, many times, women wait until they're up for partner or a managerial role to start fighting for their seat at the table, when by this time, it's often too late. If you're a woman at the beginning of your career, I challenge you to start getting your seat at the table *right now*. Once you're at the table, it's a lot harder for them to kick you away. But if you haven't been at the table, or at least striving to get there, it will be tough to find space at this table when you're more senior because, well, the table is full.

It's important for you to understand what I mean when I say "seat at the table." I don't mean this in a literal sense. A seat at the table can mean different things for different professions. I believe the only definition that carries over from profession to profession is this: a seat at the table is getting the same opportunities *at the same time* as your male counterparts. Let me say that louder, for the people in the back: *at the same time* as your male counterparts. Often, women are given the same role as a man, the same salary as a man, and the same career opportunities as a man—but *years after* their male counterparts received these. It's imperative that women not only receive these opportunities but also receive them *on time*!

Let me give you a couple of examples of what a seat at the table can look like early in your career.

Attorney. You're a young lawyer, and your male counterpart has taken a deposition in his first six months of starting at the firm. We're now at month eight, and you have no deposition in sight. If you don't take your first deposition until year two, your male counterpart has now taken four depositions compared to your one. Sure, you've both taken depositions, but he has more experience and is better at this skill than you are. Then, when you're up for partner, he's done a trial, but you haven't. He's more qualified for partner and makes partner, and you don't. You have no argument against him because you are less qualified.

When did the disparity happen? When he got his seat at the table before you. You didn't get your seat until year two; he got his six months in.

Businessperson. You're working as a team, and you start to realize that your boss, Scott, is leaving you off emails, but keeps your male counterpart, Brad, on them. The boss sometimes goes straight to Brad about portions of the project and leaves you out of these meetings. Your boss isn't being malicious; his office is next to Brad's, so it's easy to walk right to his office.

Before you know it, Brad and Scott are the best of friends and have a great natural working relationship. Scott now is Brad's mentor and sponsor and goes to bat for Brad for promotions. Thus, Brad gets more exposure than you and his career accelerates.

At what point did you miss your seat at the table? It started with the emails. At that point it was your duty to talk to Scott and Brad, informing them that, going forward, you wanted to be included on all emails regarding the project. This may seem like a small issue, but that was the moment the disparity began.

To succeed in your career and make strides, you must be at the table. But as the above examples demonstrate, you can't wait to start fighting for that seat until you're senior in your role—you have to start fighting for your seat at the table on *day one*.

Let me paint you a picture. Remember when you were a kid, and all your relatives met at one house for Thanksgiving dinner? There was the one nice, big table with fancy chairs that fit eight people. The "adult table." Then there was the folding table that lived in the basement or garage, which was brought out for special occasions: the "kids' table." At the kids' table you ate second, had the crummy fold-up chairs, used paper plates, and discussed kid things, like what was going on in school and the newest trends. At the adult table, however, you got the first slices of sweet potato pie, had deep conversations, drank wine, and ate off the fancy plates. As a kid, you always knew that one day you'd transition from the kids' table to the adult table.

Now imagine that you're twenty-five years old. You come home for the holidays and are told you must sit at the kids' table, while your twenty-five-year-old male cousin has somehow transitioned to the adult table. You immediately go to the adult table and start advocating for your position there. Their response? "I'm sorry, but there are no more chairs, and your cousin Jimmy has been asking to sit at the adult table since you guys were sixteen years old, so technically he gets first dibs."

Envision these same tables in your workplace. Your male counterparts are at the adult table (even the guy who started at your company the same day you did, ten years prior), and you and three other women are at the kids' table. How does that make you feel? If it infuriates you, I urge you to start fighting to sit at the adult table right now. Don't wait until ten years pass, and there's no space left. You have to make your superiors aware that you're serious about eventually sitting at the adult table and that you're preparing for that seat. It's your job to put them on notice. It's also your job to ensure that you're on track to transition from the kids' table to the adult table. No one will do this for you. You are the agent of your own career.

So what can you do immediately to start your transition from the kids' table to the adult table? Keep your eyes open, research, create a road map, stay aware, and advocate.

KEEP YOUR EYES OPEN AND RESEARCH

Keep your eye on the prize from day one. When you start your career, identify who the key players are. Who is at the adult table, how did they get there, and whose seat are you eyeing for yourself? After you identify the key players, do your research and find out how they made it to the adult table. Was it a lateral move? Do they have a postgraduate degree or an extra certification that you may need? Was it straight-up privilege, or did they receive a favor? Learn their journey, so you know what the road ahead entails.

CREATE A ROAD MAP

I've never seen anyone take an extended road trip without a map. I've never seen anyone bake their first cake without instructions. The same concept applies to your career—you must have a plan. Your career road map should include your career goals and how you intend to achieve them. It should also include when you hope to meet each of these goals. Remember, although important, your goals shouldn't be limited to salary and how much money you hope to make. You should include developmental goals—for example, navigating a new system, mastering new technologies, or learning new portions of the business. You should also set goals surrounding level movement (e.g., when you hope to be given a promotion).

This road map should be something you discuss with your mentor. The hope is that you create a realistic but aggressive road map. Here are a few examples of goals your career road map could include:

- I want to pass the CPA exam by year two at my company.
- I want to have a managerial role by year five.

- I want to learn how to code by year one.

Your mentor should be able to help you determine what timelines are realistic and achievable. And remember the number one rule with goals: if they aren't written down, they aren't goals—they're just dreams. We want solidified goals on paper. So, get out your pen and paper and start working on your road map.

STAY AWARE

Stay aware of what's happening in your career early on. Are you not included on emails, not invited to meetings with clients, or not given the difficult assignments, while your male counterparts are? These situations shouldn't be brushed off. They reflect unconscious bias at its core, and you have to stay aware of them, because they can ruin your career.

Implicit bias, also known as unconscious bias, is the act of judging people based on one's unconscious thoughts, beliefs, or feelings. While these biases can be completely harmless in a vacuum, implicit bias in the workplace can negatively impact decision making, from hiring to promotions.[2] Even when people have the best intentions and aren't attempting to be malicious—as in the businessperson example above—their unconscious bias can kick in.

I'll say this again in a different way: even the managers you like and respect, who also have the best intentions, can have unconscious bias that affects your career. Because the unconscious bias can come from people we like working with, we're more likely to let it slide and act like it never happened. But acting like it never happened is condoning the conduct and asking for it to happen again. The more it happens, the more you fall behind your peers, and the less likely you are to have a seat at the table.

ADVOCATE

When you start noticing you're either purposefully or inadvertently being kept at the kids' table, instead of transitioning to the adult table, you must speak up. You can do so in a few ways.

- **Get comfortable with asking uncomfortable questions.** "Hi, Scott, I noticed I was left off the email chain to the clients about the XYZ deal. Was there a particular reason, or was that just an oversight?" Imagine how easy a fix this conversation can bring about, versus being left off all the emails and then having no relationship with the client, which, in turn, means you have trouble developing business as a senior lawyer.
- **Speak up about desiring more difficult assignments.** "I noticed that Joey was given the purchase agreement to draft from scratch. In an effort to stay on par with my peers, I'm hoping you will give me the next purchase agreement assignment." You can only be your best self if you're doing the most difficult work. I guarantee you that every C-suite executive was set up for those gigs. They were put in front of clients early and given challenging

assignments. If you're not automatically getting those assignments, ask for them.

- **Document unconscious bias.** A paper trail can be powerful. When I worked at a large law firm as a junior litigator, I saved every email from partners that said I'd done a good job on a writing assignment or presented "excellent work." At my evaluation meetings, if one partner had a negative comment about my work product, I could pull out the emails, which showed that this feedback was inconsistent with the feedback from others.

MENTORS AND SPONSORS

During your journey to getting a seat at the table, you'll need two tools for success: a mentor and a sponsor. Nothing is more crucial to your success in climbing the corporate ladder than having these two people as part of your team. I'd even say that these two people outweigh, and are more important than, any specific degree, certification, or training you may receive.

Many people conflate these terms or use them interchangeably, but these are distinct roles. You're probably most familiar with the term "mentor." A mentor is defined as an "experienced and trusted adviser." For someone to be your mentor, they need three qualities: (1) have more experience than you, (2) be someone you trust, and (3) be an adviser. So, let's break this down.

First, a mentor must have more experience than you. The term "experience" is self-explanatory. You need someone who has more experience than you in the area of work you're doing. However, this doesn't mean they have to be much more experienced than you. In fact, a mentor could be someone who is just a year ahead of you on the career path. They could also be someone your exact age who just happens to have more experience than you do in the area you're seeking mentorship in.

Additionally, your mentor needs to be someone you trust. Someone with whom you can be vulnerable and are comfortable asking the "stupid" questions. And, most important, someone who won't later use your stupid questions against you. For example, let's say you ask your mentor to help you prepare a client pitch because you have no clue how to proceed. Later, a manager asks your mentor if you'd be a good person to put on a client pitch for the following month. The mentor shouldn't use against you the information he or she has. A good mentor will say, "Absolutely—that sounds like a great opportunity for Keisha. She's been working on that skill." A bad mentor will say, "I know Keisha is still working on how to pitch clients, so I don't know if she has it down yet. Maybe we skip her until the next one." True mentors see all your weaknesses in private but don't broadcast them in public.

Last, the mentor is an adviser whose sole job is to help you be better at your job. Some people refer to this as being a teacher or a coach. That could mean helping you navigate the politics in your company, teaching you how to use certain machines or systems in your field, or offering to help you negotiate your salary for your next promotion. The mentor is there to lean on, someone who has a 360-degree view of your career.

Now that you understand what a mentor is, if you don't have one, you should start looking for one. (Let's take a quick commercial break here: Although this chapter focuses on working a nine-to-five job, mentorship is critical in all walks of life. If you're an influencer, a model, a sports agent, whatever—get a mentor! Okay, back to the program.) Many companies have mentor programs where you're assigned a mentor. I find that organic mentor-mentee relationships tend to be stronger than relationships that are assigned, but a formal mentor program shouldn't be overlooked.

I took the mentor program at my law firm pretty seriously. I set up monthly coffees with my mentor as a check-in. I also sat down with my mentor and set goals for the year. I shared each of these goals with my mentor, to determine how realistic they were. I then used those goals as mile markers reflecting where I was in my career and how I was doing. My coffees with my mentor typically involved me explaining what I'd done to get closer to my goals and the mistakes I'd made along the way. I put a lot of work into the formal mentor program and made it work for me. I didn't wait for my mentor to set up check-ins. I took the initiative and made sure they happened.

CHOOSING A MENTOR

Choose your mentor wisely. My biggest recommendation when choosing a mentor is to look for someone who didn't drink the company Kool-Aid. You need a mentor who's truly vested in your career and what's best for you, not what's best for the company. It can be dangerous to have a mentor who's too big of a cheerleader for the company, because their opinions and advice will typically be one-sided and biased.

Some of the best advice I've ever received from a mentor was that I needed to make a lateral move, or I'd be better off at a competitor. A person who drank the company Kool-Aid won't be able to give you that type of advice. Also, you can have a mentor from outside your company. Some of the strongest mentor relationships are formed at networking events, where two professionals in the same industry meet up in a relaxed setting.

SPONSORSHIP

Now, let's talk about a sponsor. As much as I believe a mentor is important for a successful career, a sponsor is perhaps even more important. If I had to have only one, either a mentor or a sponsor, I'd choose a sponsor in a heartbeat. What's the difference? In short, a mentor advises, whereas a sponsor advocates. Sponsors take a direct role in the advancement of the protégé—you.[3]

A sponsor is a career champion. Unlike a mentor, a sponsor must be at your company. Also unlike a mentor, a sponsor cannot be your peer. Instead, a sponsor is a senior-level staff member. Someone who's in the room and already has a seat at the table. Someone who has the ability to put skin in the game on your behalf. Someone who has connections in your company to assist in advancing your career. Someone who can beat on the table and advocate for you when you're not in the room. Someone who has clout and/or pull within the company.

In addition, "sponsors promote protégés directly, using their influence and networks to connect them to high-profile assignments, people, pay increases, and promotions. . . . Sponsors champion their protégés' visibility, often using their own platforms and reputation as a medium for exposure."[4] Sponsors put their name on the line for their protégés.

If you are still confused about what a sponsor is or how critical they can be to an employee's success, take a step back and look at the senior-level employees at your company. I bet you can think of, or you can ask them, what single person helped the trajectory of their career. Or ask, if they could identify only one person to attribute some of their success, who would that person be? That person is likely their sponsor.

HOW TO FIND A SPONSOR

It's imperative to have a sponsor, especially for minorities and women. As stated above, you need someone who has a seat at the table and can advocate for your success when you're not in the room.

When I teach about sponsors, I'm consistently asked the same question: "We get it—sponsors are important. But how do we get one?" This is the hard part. In a perfect world, a sponsor would choose you as a protégé. A sponsor would see something in you that he or she related to and therefore gravitate toward you. But since the sponsor needs to be in a power position, and minorities and women don't always secure those positions, we often see women and minorities lacking the much-needed sponsorship. It goes back to unconscious bias, a barrier to workplace success. Humans are naturally drawn to and trust people who look like them or have things in common with them. Humans are also more likely to advocate for people who look like them. According to a LeanIn.Org and McKinsey & Company report, 66 percent of all C-suite executives at the companies surveyed are white men,[5] so as you can see, it's that much harder for minorities and women to get a sponsor.

This is where sponsoring yourself comes into play.

HOW TO SPONSOR YOURSELF

While you're waiting for a sponsor to come your way, you can sponsor yourself.

Keep a record. While working in corporate America, you can easily forget some of the kick-butt things you've done for a company or in your career. Because of this, I recommend you always keep a record! When you start a new job, buy a journal to keep on your desk and track everything good you've done for your company. You should include every charity event or luncheon you attend and which manager had requested your attendance. You should also keep a list of every substantial or difficult project you worked on and completed. As well as any additional continuing education seminars or extra certifications you obtain. Additionally, you should keep an email folder on your computer, to save all emails you receive that include good feedback or praise.

When it comes time for your annual review, you should be prepared to advocate in the room why you deserve that raise, that promotion, or that new title. Go back to your journal and review all of the things you accomplished in the last year and include those in your self-evaluation to your manager.

Let me take a second here to just talk to the ladies. For whatever reason, women can be so self-deprecating. We never want to brag on ourselves, for fear of coming off cocky. News flash: most men will brag on themselves in a heartbeat! And bragging on yourself when you're simply listing facts isn't being cocky; it's stating your value. If you don't have written self-evaluations, bring your work journal to your review to make sure you remember everything you'd accomplished that year.

Let me give you a tip about writing self-evaluations. Write them like you are writing a recommendation letter for a friend. Write it in third person to ensure you do not hold anything back. Here's an example: "Christine has been a phenomenal associate. She has written every type of motion and even participated in trial." After you finish the letter, go back and rewrite the letter, replacing your friend's name with *I.* "I have been a phenomenal associate. I have written every type of motion and even participated in trial." See how this strategy allows you to be more specific and complimentary? Just like we comment on our friend's Instagram post ("yes, girl, *hair!*"), it should be that easy to applaud ourselves. Put that same energy into your review.

Show, don't tell. A partner at my law firm often told young associates to "show, don't tell" when writing motions. It took me forever to understand this concept in writing and advocating, but now I see how beneficial it can be. For instance, instead of saying, "Nicole Lynn represents some of the best athletes in the world" (which is me *telling* you), say, "Nicole Lynn represents Erik Harris of the Raiders, Jordan Evans of the Bengals, and Quinnen Williams of the Jets" (which is me *showing* you).

Show the reader what you did by using examples and facts. Instead of saying, "Sally is a hard worker," say, "Sally took on additional projects that her peers turned down. Sally came in early and stayed late on several occasions." Saying "Sally is a hard worker" provides no evidence for this assertion. When writing a self-evaluation or advocating for a raise or promotion, make sure you *show* and don't tell.

AGENT YOU: TAKE ACTION!

1. Get a seat at the table, *now.* Remember the five ways to secure your place:

    - *Keep your eyes open and research.* Who is at the table, and how did they get there? What can you learn from their journey that benefits you?
    - *Create a road map.* Make a list of your career goals and how you will achieve them. Think beyond salary to what all aspects of success look like for you.
    - *Stay aware.* Pay attention to how you're being treated, especially in relation to peers with the same level of experience as you.
    - *Advocate.* This is threefold: (1) Get comfortable asking uncomfortable questions. (2) Speak up about desiring more difficult assignments. (3) Document unconscious bias.

2. Choose a mentor. Recall the three criteria for a mentor, who should be (1) more experienced than you, (2) someone you trust, and (3) an adviser.

- Make a list of at least five people you think could mentor you.
- What specific benefits would each person bring to the relationship? For example, do they possess a skill set you want or need to learn to advance in your career? Or have they excelled in their career while also maintaining a healthy work-life balance?
- To narrow down your selection, you might also find it helpful to make a list of pros and cons for each person on the list.

3. Find a sponsor. You become someone's protégé, because that person can advocate for you and leverage connections to get you where you want to go.

- List at least five potential sponsors.
- As with your mentors list, identify what specific benefits each person would bring to the relationship. Are they respected and admired by many people both inside and outside of your company? Do they have connections to clients or industry insiders who could greatly boost your career?
- Also similar to your mentor search, you can list pros and cons for each person on your potential sponsor list.
- If you can't find a sponsor right away, sponsor yourself! Keep a work journal where you record all your accomplishments, and practice showing instead of telling when you promote yourself.

Don't wait—fight for your
seat at the table today.

CHAPTER ELEVEN

Practice Self-Care

W hen I originally conceptualized this book, it was solely focused on the reader finding purpose in life and how to be successful in that purpose. But then, as I began to write this book, I reflected on my own life. I absolutely was walking in purpose, no question. I've almost always known what I wanted to do in life. I'd taken the jump to get there, worked hard and made the necessary sacrifices, passed the "purpose test," and was now living in my self-defined "success." Even with all I'd accomplished in life, I realized a hard truth: I still wasn't happy.

My mom said, "Happiness is dictated by what is *happening* around you (happening = happiness), but joy surpasses any circumstance. Pray for joy, not happiness." Frankly, I didn't have either. I wanted so badly to enjoy the fruits of my work, but something was off.

"If you love what you do, you'll never work a day in your life." I believed that with my whole heart.

I then learned that you work your whole life to succeed, and even when you hit that success, it doesn't automatically bring you happiness or peace. What a letdown. My journey toward finding peace is ongoing. For those of you who are like me, still searching for peace—this chapter is for you. Step one of finding or regaining your peace is making sure you take care of yourself. Know that even as I share the insights I've learned over the years, I'm there on the path right next to you.

•   •   •

First, let's get something important out of the way. I've just spent ten chapters telling you that you need to work harder than everyone else and make tremendous sacrifices to reach your goals. Now, I'm telling you to prioritize self-care. So which is it?

The answer to that question is both.

Working hard and practicing self-care aren't mutually exclusive, though we often think of them that way. Even so, the time and effort (or money) you're able to dedicate to self-care efforts won't always be the same. For instance, when I've been at the height of the hustle, I might not have been able to manage much in the way of self-care. A spa day would have been out of the question (and frankly, undesirable), but I could certainly do something like take five minutes out of my day to jot down a gratitude list or sip a mug of tea while staring out a window and listening to some of my favorite slow jams.

Self-care is one of the biggest trends right now. Many podcasters, motivational speakers, and influencers are completely focused on discussing this topic. Overworking yourself and not putting yourself first is probably the least cool thing you can do today. But just because this new self-care culture has arisen and totally infiltrated our lives doesn't mean we shouldn't take it seriously.

I think about self-care the same way I think about the Super Bowl halftime show. This highly anticipated event is one of the most-watched performances of the year. Millions of viewers tune in for those twenty minutes. However, many fans don't realize that halftime wasn't put in place for entertainment—it was intended to give players a chance to take a break and regroup. I think about halftime as the players' opportunity for self-care. We all must take "halftimes" in our life, just like professional athletes do in the middle of a game. Unfortunately, people like me tend to skip halftime and go right from the second to the third quarter. When you're an agent for your own life, it's crucial that you take your halftime seriously.

I've always been bad about taking halftimes and have paid the price for it over and over, such as when I had my first nervous breakdown. I vividly remember the mental, physical, and emotional exhaustion. I'd traveled across the country for two back-to-back NFL games for my players. In between these games, I filmed a commercial for NFL Network, met with my players' families, and recorded a podcast, all while drafting motions for my legal job. I got home and fell to my knees. "Something's got to give," I cried to myself. I was working two jobs, with twenty-five clients who all needed me constantly, and was suffering from severe anxiety and sleep deprivation. I was working myself to death and was too afraid to get help. (Sis, can we talk about the mental health stigma? My gosh . . .)

Since halftimes don't come naturally to me, this was a skill I needed to learn and perfect, just like dancing or playing a sport. I also had to change my perspective on halftimes and recognize that they're not a reward and are nonnegotiable. Agent Nicole Lynn is only as successful as the halftimes she allows herself to take. The same goes for you.

Let's deep dive into what a halftime looks like and explore how your life can drastically change when you prioritize this practice.

TAKING CARE OF YOU

Of all the chapters in this book, this was the most difficult one to write. Unlike many of the other topics in this book, I have consistently failed at this chapter's topic, self-care, day in and day out. How do people who are always on prioritize something like self-care? The short answer is: they don't. I honestly didn't realize how bad I was at self-care until I tried it. At first, I had no idea what self-care looked like, and when I did learn what it looked like I never made time for it, or when I had the time, I couldn't get myself to do it. It was a big whirlwind of disaster.

When I finally realized this wasn't something I could master on my own, I sought advice from a couple of friends who took self-care seriously. I also read a ton of books and blogs, and listened to several podcasts on the topic. Some of the information was helpful, but most wasn't. After trial and error,

I decided that I was doing this self-care thing all wrong—and maybe you are too.

DON'T START WITH ACTIONS

When struggling to master the art of self-care (because it is an art), you shouldn't start with booking spa days and taking vacations. Trust me—I've tried that. For my first self-care attempt, I did what most amateurs do: I booked a massage. The experience was horrible. My mind was racing the entire time. Mentally, I kept going through my to-do list, reorganizing my budget, and wondering how much time was left in the massage. I left feeling more anxious than when I'd walked in. I wasn't sure what this "self-care" was supposed to do for me, but I didn't feel any better. In fact, I beat myself up because of the amount of time I'd wasted that I could have spent doing more productive things.

After this experience, I realized this: *you cannot start your self-care journey with action.* Instead, you first have to change your mindset about how you view self-care as a whole. Because I'm programmed to be "on" at all times, in order to be effective at self-care, I had to learn to be okay with temporarily being "off." The journey to change my mindset and view about self-care was a long one, and I'm still on it today.

My first step was learning how to simply exist.

EXISTING

There is something so powerful in being able to just exist. For someone like me—and for many of you—we believe our life has a purpose and all our actions have meaning. Many of the decisions we make on a daily basis are in an effort to achieve said purpose. Every move we make is for the greater goal. We work to be the best at what we do, because we feel we've been called to be the best.

Additionally, it seems that it's no longer okay to merely work a "regular" job—everyone must have a side hustle, a business, a blog, a nonprofit, or something else to brag about at happy hour. The world is evolving from the days when being a lawyer was enough. Now you must be a lawyer *and* fight injustice. Gone are the days when being a teacher was sufficient. Now you must be a teacher *and* your students' salvation, like the teacher in the movie *Freedom Writers*. And it's no longer okay just to be a stay-at-home mom. You also must be PTA president, the soccer mom with the best snacks, and MVP of all moms. This is the new normal.

As the world has created these new norms, there is power in the ability to just exist. Exist in your role as a marketing rep. Exist in your role as a consultant. Exist in your role as a nurse. Exist in your role as a mom or dad. To the select group of people who can just exist and be comfortable with that, I commend you. For many, however, just existing can cause fear and anxiety. We think, *If I'm not aiming for a greater purpose, with a million goals ahead of me, then what's the point of my life?*

Those who don't experience this inner turmoil have a completely different experience. They go to work, come home, enjoy their friends and family, eat their favorite foods, relax, and are perfectly satisfied with their daily contribution to society. If this is you, let me be the first to tell you this is extremely impressive. Based on my observation, the people who can just exist and who avoid conforming to the new societal norms seem to have more peace.

A lot of people have mastered the ability to just exist in isolated moments. These people are still striving to determine their greater purpose or are working hard toward achieving their purpose, but can "turn it off" at times, to take a moment for themselves. This group of people can be still and be present.

BEING OKAY WITH DOING NOTHING

So, how does existing correlate to self-care? I truly believe the first step in tackling issues with self-care is learning to be okay with just existing. In other words, being okay with doing nothing. Brené Brown calls it white space. Stuart Brown calls it "time spent without purpose."[1] Whatever you call it, it's not easy for everyone. For some of you reading this, you're thinking: *What's the big deal? Just get your massage and relax.* But for others, this is one of the most difficult tasks you'll face on your journey to find peace.

Once you change your mindset, you're more likely to enjoy self-care and have less anxiety surrounding the actual action. It may take you a long time to be okay with letting time pass without purpose or being okay with blank space, but stay the course. Do not move to implementing self-care actions until you can master this mindset change.

For those who struggle with self-care, when you have an open slot on your calendar, don't fill the time with reading a book, getting a massage, or pampering yourself (although all are great self-care tools to be used further down the path). Instead, fill the time with existing. Write in your planner that on Tuesday from 10:00 to 10:30 a.m., you will simply exist.

I remember vacationing in Jamaica, lying out on the beach, and realizing my audiobook hadn't downloaded. All I could think about was the amount of time wasted lounging on the beach, when I could have been listening to my book. So, as plan B, I laid on the beach and planned out the next two days in Jamaica, while also brainstorming new ways to recruit clients. Sadly, I was unable to just exist in that moment. To just be present. Those who master the art of existing are no longer slaves to to-do lists. They also don't equate existing with wasting time.

Practice makes perfect. I challenge you to learn to just exist by practicing daily. Every day, set aside ten minutes to just exist. Sit on the couch without your phone, pause in the car before going in the house from work, or lie in bed and stare at the ceiling. Some would call this quiet time or meditation, but I think both of those are vastly different. Quiet time is usually equated with some sort of spiritual or religious moment, as in quiet time with God. Meditation is engaging in a mental exercise, usually while focusing on one's breathing. Both quiet time and meditation have end goals in mind. Existing does not. The only goals, if you will, are to be present in the moment and be okay that all you're doing is existing.

In addition to the ten minutes daily, incorporate one longer session of existing each week, for thirty minutes to an hour. Eventually, this time will be replaced with a self-care action, but not until you're able to understand and experience the deeper concept of existing. When you walk into your planned "existing time," remind yourself: *I am not reflecting. I am not spending time with God. I am not meditating. I am not getting alone time. I am not thinking. I am not relaxing. I am merely existing.* And do your best to be okay with that.

After mastering the art of existing, you can step into the action portion of self-care. Start replacing your "existing" time with self-care activities. Self-care comes in all forms, and we'll touch on a number of them. But first, let's discuss why self-care is important and why it truly contributes to living your best life.

You have to take care of you. When working long nights at the law firm, another attorney once told me, "This law firm will take every ounce that you give it." I believe that applies in all industries and all walks of life. Life will continue to take from you, over and over, more and more. At some point, life will take everything you have, because the inevitable will happen: you will die. Until then, it's your job to limit how much life can take from you while you're alive. It's your job to set boundaries on life. It's not only your job—it's one of the most important jobs you'll ever have. And this is where self-care comes into play: it helps you set boundaries.

As I've mentioned, I'm still weak in this area, but I'm continually striving to improve. It's a vulnerable space for me, as I can never seem to get it right to my satisfaction. But because I recognize how important self-care is, I'll never stop attempting to master it.

Self-care comes in all shapes and sizes. Though there's no one-size-fits-all approach, there are a few key takeaways that all moments of self-care should include:

1. Self-care must be done consistently.
2. Self-care should not be viewed as a reward.
3. Self-care is nonnegotiable.
4. The strongest people take self-care seriously.

Self-care must be done consistently. Self-care isn't something that should be done when you can make time or when you feel like it. Instead, it should be an integral part of your routine. If you're a literal person like me, someone who needs goals and checkmarks, then it's important to intentionally set aside time for self-care. The easiest way to do this is to put it on your schedule, just like you'd do with any other priority. I feel that self-care should be done daily, with extended time on a weekly basis, similar to your "existing" time. It should be as consistent as brushing your teeth and become second nature.

Self-care should not be viewed as a reward. Think of it this way: a shower or bath may feel amazing after a long workout, but it's not a reward for working out—it's a necessary task that happens to follow a tough task. If you view self-care as a priority instead of as a reward, this perspective will help you incorporate it into your everyday life. When you view self-care as a reward, two things happen: (1) you run the risk of adding guilt to your self-care, and (2) it becomes something that's not taken seriously, thus allowing it to be skipped.

When I think of a reward system, I think of allowing myself something that's normally prohibited. For example, rewarding yourself with a piece of chocolate cake after a long week of clean eating. No matter how much you may deserve that chocolate cake, and no matter how hard you worked for it, there's usually some level of guilt associated with it. This can happen with self-care. If you view these actions as rewards, you run the risk of feeling guilty when you commit to them.

I'm not a rewards type of person. I work hard because I believe we're supposed to, not because of some arbitrary reward we receive from doing so. However, because of my sometimes skewed way of thinking, I'm more likely to skip something that looks like a reward. Instead, if my mind thinks something is a priority or essential to life, I'm more likely to remain consistent with it. It's all about perspective and knowing yourself.

I've sometimes had to trick myself into self-care with some of these tactics. Think of self-care as no more or less important or fun than any other kind of routine personal maintenance. It's something you have to do and need to do and that cannot be skipped under any circumstances.

Self-care is nonnegotiable. In writing this section, I feel like a huge hypocrite for what I am about to say. But, hey, here we go! Self-care is nonnegotiable, and any person or thing that interferes with your consistent self-care should be removed from your life. I have often allowed people, jobs, and activities to stick around in my life, even though I knew these were hindering me from taking care of myself. It's hard; I get it. Yet the trade-off isn't worth it.

If you were working at a job and they said you couldn't eat for a week straight, would you keep that job? If you had a boyfriend who said you couldn't take the medicine that you needed to stay alive, would that boyfriend still be in your life? Self-care needs to be as nonnegotiable as other tasks, like eating, that keep you alive.

The strongest people take self-care seriously. I spent the majority of my life associating the need for self-care with weakness. You know, those people who say no to things because they had "too much on their plate." The people who *needed* alone time to "recharge." Those people who set boundaries and value work-life balance. Yeah, *those* people. Those people were not me. I never understood what the big deal was. I had the mentality that you sleep when you're dead and work while you're young. This very dangerous attitude dictated my entire twenties. Although a work-hard mentality can be beneficial, it can also be extremely detrimental. *Those* people got it. They understood that the phrase "work hard, play hard" meant that play had to be part of the equation. Don't believe the hype—a hype I unfortunately sold and lived by for more than a decade. Working hard is important, but work-life balance is essential.

DAILY SELF-CARE

What does self-care look like on a daily basis? For me, I needed specific examples of what people were doing for self-care. Here's a short list to get you started:

- Get a massage.
- Take a trip with friends.
- Get your nails done.
- See a therapist.
- Hire a cleaning person.
- Deep condition your hair.
- Take a walk around your neighborhood.

All of these are great self-care tools, and most are things you can do on a weekly, monthly, or quarterly basis. But because I believe self-care needs to be daily, I started brainstorming smaller-scale self-care ideas. The following are a few examples:

- Spend an extra two minutes in the shower, allowing the hot water to roll down your body while you just exist.
- Listen to your favorite song in the car from start to finish before walking in to work.
- Watch a Netflix show before bed.
- Read a few pages of your favorite book.
- Eat a small piece of chocolate midday as a pick-me-up.
- Turn your phone off.
- Take a fifteen-minute power nap.
- Take a break from social media.

These tasks can seem so mundane that they're unimportant. But even when reading that list of daily self-care suggestions, I'm shocked that I could go a week without doing a single one. They're not natural for me. Can you relate? I take a shower and quickly jump out because I have places to go. I rarely take naps. I view chocolate as a reward, or even worse, as a part of my "cheat day." Unless I deliberately choose to do these things, none will just sneak into my daily life. We must be intentional about adding the small actions, which are sometimes the most powerful, as they build up over time.

Accountability. One way to ensure you stay on track is to keep yourself accountable by journaling your self-care. Journaling your self-care can be eye-opening. It not only ensures that you do it, it also provides a track record to remind you that you're on your way. Going back and reading, "Tuesday: Painted my nails while listening to Ariana Grande's 'Dangerous Woman,'" lets you know you're making progress. It also gives you ideas when you forget what self-care you've done in the past, as well as what worked and what still felt like a task.

In your journal, write exactly how the self-care feels, good or bad. For example, "I did *X* today for self-care. Still felt like work," or "Watched an episode of *Grey's Anatomy*. Clients kept texting me during the show. Next time, I'll try watching the show with phone on 'do not disturb.'" Keep yourself accountable with self-care the same way you would with a workout or healthy eating (which are both forms of self-care, by the way).

Protect Your Self-Care. One of my close friends, Christine, protects her self-care time like she would a baby. She used to tell me: "I'm sorry. I can't do *X* because I have to protect my time today, since it's my off day."

My response? "What do you mean 'protect your time'? No one is stealing your time." I thought her statement was one of the most absurd things I'd ever heard in my life. She was telling me she couldn't run errands with me because she planned to sit in her room the entire day, binge-watching *Power*? I didn't get it. She treated self-care the same way I treated a big meeting at my corporate job. Just as I would say: "Sorry, I've got to run. I have a huge meeting with the CEO of my company in fifteen minutes and will be out of pocket for two hours. Will call you after," she would say almost the identical thing when protecting her self-care.

Fast-forward several years later, and I no longer think she's crazy. She learned early on that self-care was a priority, not a reward. She also made it a priority that was *equal* to all her other priorities.

It's important for you to protect your self-care time—to put it on your calendar and let nothing, outside of an emergency, take away this time. When you begin to protect your self-care time, others will do the same. As my friend continually told me about her Self-Care Sundays, I stopped asking her to do things on Sundays. I started to naturally respect her time and even found myself telling others: "I know Christine isn't available during that time. Can we push to Monday?" She communicated that her self-care time was crucial, so I respected that boundary and even helped her maintain it by communicating it to others.

When you first start protecting your self-care time, know that some people won't take your effort seriously. Don't let their comments affect your goal. You're investing in the most important thing on this planet: *you*. There is nothing trivial, frivolous, or minor about this.

AGENT YOU:
TAKE ACTION!

1. Be okay with doing nothing. You can't start your self-care journey with actions. Begin by being okay with just existing. This doesn't come naturally to many people, but keep practicing.

2. Practice self-care. Self-care looks different for everyone, and it might take time for you to find activities that work for you.

   - Make a list of at least five ways you can practice daily self-care.
   - Now, list several ways you can practice weekly or monthly self-care.
   - Journal your self-care experiences, to hold yourself accountable and to ensure that your self-care activities don't feel like another item you have to check off your to-do list.

3. Protect your self-care time. Life will continually take from you, so if you don't fiercely guard your self-care sessions, something will consume that time.

- After you've identified ways you can practice self-care, block off the necessary time on your calendar, and make these appointments with yourself nonnegotiable.
- Don't be afraid to communicate these boundaries to others. If they respect you, they'll respect your self-care boundaries.

Self-care is a priority,
not a reward.

CHAPTER TWELVE

Let Go of Busy

t's finals week in my first year of law school. I am a wreck. I haven't slept in days and my anxiety is off the charts. I've made a schedule for each day, with how many hours I will study for each final. I am adamant about following this schedule. At this point in my life, law school and my class rank are the most important things to me. My priorities are, in order: law school, good grades, get a job, be successful.

I'm sitting in front of the computer, working on my law school final's outline, and my phone rings. It's my half-brother Vincent Jr., whom we all call Cooda. *I wonder what he wants,* I think as I answer the phone.

"Hey, what's up?" I say, in an annoyed/rushed voice.

"Big sis, I'm trying to come live with you. I need to get out of Tulsa. Can I come live with you? I want to turn my life around."

I sigh. "Cooda, I'm in the middle of finals. Can you call me next week, and we can talk about it then?" We exchange some quick pleasantries and I hang up. The next day he calls me again. This time I decline. I am too busy to answer, and my first final is a day away. The following day, the day of my final, he calls again. *What does he want?* I wonder as I once again decline his call.

• • •

As I walk out after my last final, I think: *I'm finished! I'm free!*

That night, my husband takes me to dinner to celebrate my birthday, which had happened during finals week, and to celebrate finishing my first semester of law school. We go to The Cheesecake Factory. We sit in a booth, because I always sit in booths. One of my closest friends and her boyfriend drive into town to surprise me.

The night couldn't be more perfect. I'm finally done with my first semester of law school, and I'm celebrating my birthday with my favorite people.

While we're waiting for our food to come out, my phone rings. It's Julius, my other brother. I assume he's calling to wish me happy birthday, so I answer right there at the table.

"Cooda's dead, Nikki. They shot Cooda," he screams. He's crying and inconsolable, wailing.

I yell at my husband to let me out of the booth, and I run to the bathroom. *How could this have happened? How could they have killed my brother?* My husband follows me to the bathroom and holds me in his arms as I cry my eyes out. I try not to vomit. I can't see straight and think I might pass out. My mind races, and then it hits me:

He had called me that day, and I ignored his call. I was too busy.

See, the thing about me is that I am *always* too busy. I don't mean a little busy. I mean, back-to-back meetings, travel every weekend, a to-do list longer than anyone I know type of busy. When my friends think of me, the first thought that comes to mind is that I am probably working. I work *really* hard. When you grow up in poverty, like I did, you have no choice but to work hard. I have had a job since I was fourteen years old. I have consistently worked harder than my peers and, because of my hard work, have gotten to places in life that others could only dream of. I am where I am because of two things: the favor of God and my work ethic.

But this chapter isn't a motivational speech on how to work harder—it's quite the contrary. My work ethic has been both my best and worst quality to date. And although I've had major success because of it, being busy has come at a high cost and has sometimes cost more than I was willing to pay. That's the part no one talks about.

People aren't bragging on social media about the negative side effects of the hustle. On Instagram, you may see a post of someone "grinding" at 3:00 a.m., but what you don't see is that this person suffers from chronic insomnia. You may see another commenting on being "booked and busy," but behind the scenes he or she suffers from crippling anxiety at the thought of the to-do list.

Let me be the first to give you the inside scoop and implore you not to fall into the hustle trap.

THE HUSTLE

If I can give you one piece of advice about working hard, it's this: *stop glorifying the hustle.* And I am speaking to myself on this one. Being a hustler is a huge part of our culture. If you aren't a hustler and you don't have fifty million jobs, a blog, and a side hustle, you aren't good enough. It's a toxic way of thinking. The harder you work, the more the world cheers, which then makes you work even harder. It's a vicious cycle that forces us to push our bodies and our minds beyond limits they were never created to go. We praise those who don't take breaks, who sleep in their office, and who never take vacations. Working hard becomes less about actually getting work done, and more about maintaining the status that comes with it. At least, that's how it was for me.

Working hard became so much a part of who I was that it *was* my identity. If I wasn't working hard, I wasn't myself. I found a sense of accomplishment in never taking breaks. In being able to push myself past limits that my peers couldn't. It became natural for me to say, "Oh, I'm so busy," or "Oh, I have so much to do." I wasn't lying; I *was* so busy, and I *did* have so much to do. But a lot of my hard work was out of habit, because overworking myself was instilled into my brain as "the only way."

I still think about the missed call and how I was too busy for my brother. How I will never get that moment back. I wonder, *If I had just been less busy, would he be alive?* The truth is, my brother grew up in circumstances that no one should have to endure. He was a product of his surroundings and a broken system. Gang affiliation was prevalent in the town I grew up in, and it was a dangerous place. So, if I'd answered that call, would it have changed the outcome? I'm not sure. But I do know that I never want to have to ask myself that question again.

It took me several years to forgive myself, and now I experience a lot of anxiety anytime a family member calls. Even when I'm genuinely unable to answer the phone, I fear I'll regret that decision later.

I never want to be "too busy" again. I want to have my priorities in line, so I don't have to question whether I'm too busy for something. I don't want to be thought of as Nicole Lynn, the person who always works. I don't want you to think of me and only think of my jobs. I want to stop glorifying the hustle, and instead glorify the hustlers who can balance the grind with grace. It's time that we all "let go of busy."

HOW TO LET GO OF BUSY

Don't be part of the problem.
I am part of the problem. Honestly, I created the problem. I am a founding father of the freaking problem. Let me tell you why. If you go look at my social media right now, you won't see a single photo of me having drinks with friends, or me vacationing, or me getting a pedicure. My pictures are almost solely about work—working hard and the success I've achieved from working hard. And if you want to get to where I am, the only route I show involves overworking. I am constantly celebrating my own hard work, and many of you are too.

To stop the cycle, we must stop validating people (including me) for overworking. Let's find other ways to celebrate people and their work. Instead of saying, "Girl, she is a hard worker—she works herself to death," how about saying, "Wow, she is a creative genius," "She is an amazing networker," or "She is excellent at what she does"? Part of letting go of busy is letting go of the celebration of overworking. Remember, there is a huge difference between hard work and overworking; do not confuse the two.

Work smart, not hard.
I always work hard, but I don't always work smart. I am a checkmark person. If a list of things need to be completed before checking them off, I'll do every single thing on that list, even if it isn't helpful.

For instance, when I was studying for the bar exam, the course I signed up for provided a list of things you should be doing every day for ten weeks. Four weeks into studying, I realized that one task wasn't conducive to my learning style and wasn't helpful. But because I was working hard and not smart, I still spent three hours on this specific task every day, just so I could complete everything on the list.

This example is the epitome of working hard and not smart. Working smart is all about saving yourself time and doing things that move you toward the goal. It doesn't matter how you reach the goal, as long as you get there efficiently.

During my time studying for the bar exam, I also realized I feared telling people I only finished 90 percent of the bar study program instead of 100 percent, because then it might seem like I wasn't the hard worker everyone believed I was. Even missing 10 percent of the assignments because they weren't helpful could make people think I was a slacker. Do you follow my thought process? I was hurting myself and doing unnecessary work (while putting myself at a disadvantage) for fear of not living up to my "identity" as a hard worker. Can we talk about a toxic trait?

I challenge my busy bee readers: if there's anything you're doing solely for the sake of working hard, stop now. Do you arrive at your office earlier than everyone so you can be first, even though no one is there to see you? Do you find yourself logging back in at night so you can get a head start, even though nothing is "due" anytime soon? Do you take on every assignment that comes your way and join every committee, even though you *know* you don't have time?

Take a moment and analyze your life: *What things am I working too hard on? Is there a way to be more efficient? More resourceful?* Let's let go of busy and work smarter.

Get your priorities in line.

If you want to stop being busy, you have to get your priorities in line. Your priorities are like juggling balls. One ball may be your work, another your marriage, another your friends, another a hobby, and so on. As you are juggling all these priorities and adding more along the way, one of those balls is going to fall. Even professional jugglers can only juggle so many items until one of them accidentally slips and hits the floor. Now imagine you are the juggler. Which of these balls of life will you *not* allow to fall, regardless of whether the others do? That is how you identify your priorities.

For me, even if everything else is crashing and burning and all of my balls are on the ground, my job will always still be in the air. That shows that my job is my number one priority. That's not something I'm proud of, but it's the truth. My marriage could be crashing and burning, while I'm negotiating massive NFL deals and signing top players. (This almost did happen, but that's a story for another book.)

Take a moment and think about your priorities. Are these priorities something you'll be proud of at the end of your life? I doubt that anyone's last words were "I wish I would have worked more." And it's important to have holistic priorities. This may include your profession in some capacity, but it should also include whatever else matters to you—faith, family, marriage, kids, friends, yourself, community, and so forth. There is no value in being "busy" all your life if you're not working toward a life you're proud of living. Otherwise, you're simply a hamster on a wheel, neglecting other values and going nowhere fast. Get your priorities in line, so you can dictate which assignments/tasks/favors you take on and which ones you let go.

Learn how to say no to what throws your priorities off.
I am a yes person. I almost always say yes, and when I absolutely have to say no, I find ways to put it off. It's never, "Sorry, I can't attend," but "I need to check my calendar and get back to you," knowing dang well my calendar is right in front of me and fully booked. Or "I am not 100 percent sure yet, but will get back to you." Get back to you for what? I already know the answer is that I can't.

I had to teach myself how to say no. And even when I finally mustered the courage to say no, I had immediate regrets. But here's the good news: when I did convince myself to say no, the regret eventually subsided and I still maintained my free time and my peace (bonus points are always given for retaining your peace).

I have a tip for you: Start with no. When someone asks you to do something, assume it will be a no and then work backward. For example, someone emails you to speak on a panel. Your first thought shouldn't be, *Sure, I can do this unless it's inconvenient or doesn't work.* Your first thought should be, *No, I won't be participating in this unless it makes sense for me.* Start with the no. This way of thinking requires you to identify exactly why you're accepting an invitation or saying yes to a favor, rather than why you are not. Let's look at a few examples.

- Someone asks: Can you take on this additional assignment? You think: No, unless it aligns with my career goals and I have time.
- Someone asks: Can you volunteer this weekend at a work event? You think: No, unless I have another day off and have absolutely nothing else to do.
- Someone asks: Do you want to attend this happy hour with me? You think: No, unless there will be people there I want to see and it sounds like a fun time.

When you start with no, it changes the way you view decision making. Remember, it's not about saying no—it's about deciding if and when you're going to say yes. It's a lot easier to have an internal battle with yourself about whether you should say yes than whether you should say no. Working backward and starting with no helps with this. It may feel counterintuitive at first, but doing so will eventually help you normalize the word *no* in your vocabulary.

Evaluate what needs to be done versus what you want to get done.

Everything is *not* an emergency. People who stay busy believe that everything is due today. Everything, with or without a deadline, is urgent and must be completed ASAP. When you feel extremely busy, take a moment to determine what you *need* to get done versus what you *want* to get done. Type A personalities (the busy bees) like to get through as many items on their to-do list as possible. Thus, they'll try to complete as many tasks in a day as they can.

When you find yourself knee-deep in work, you should rearrange your to-do list. Here's one way to do it: Grab two sheets of paper. On the first page, write down everything you need to do, whether a need or want. (I find I'm more productive when my to-do list is visual.) Then, cross off every nonurgent task and write these on the second piece of separate paper. Now you have two lists—one with important things you *need* to get done and one with things you *want* to get done, but can wait. Work your way down the "need" list and only move to the "want" list when all the needs are done *and* if you have extra time.

Do what you need for yourself first.

Yesterday, I had every intention to finish writing this chapter. But first, I needed to finish negotiating an NFL contract, cite check a response motion for my attorney job, help a player order furniture for his new place, and take a bunch of calls, among other things. Today, I decided that I wouldn't let anything interfere with finishing this chapter, and the only way to do that was to wake up early and do it first.

Do things for you first. When you're a hustler and a busy bee, you tend to put everything that needs to be done for others or for work before yourself. Then, at the end of your day, you find you haven't done a single thing for *you.* Because of this, when a new day begins, it's important to see to our own needs first.

Each night, set out your goals for the next day, including things you want to do for yourself. Here were my goals for today that were 100 percent for myself: finish this chapter in my book, do a thirty-minute workout, and watch an episode of *90 Day Fiancé*—my new guilty pleasure. I decided I'd wake up early and, before I touched a single thing for my job or my clients, I'd knock out the things that I'd planned for myself.

To get these things done, I have to wake up earlier than I normally would, so I have the free time to dedicate to myself before the world needs me. For someone who isn't a morning person, this is anything but easy. I would much rather stay up and work late than get up early to work. But when I do stay up late, I usually don't turn to things for myself until dead last in the day. Then I'm fighting sleep and exhausted and not giving 110 percent to things that matter most: the things for me. By waking up early and tackling self-care first, I reinforce that I'm the most important thing on my to-do list.

I used to laugh at people who woke up at 5:00 a.m. to work out. I actually hated those people and their cheery Instagram posts about how good they feel because they worked out, showered, and are already drinking a cup of coffee, and it's only 7:00 a.m. (*Who cares, Sally? I am still asleep.*) But these very people who drove me crazy are the ones who get it. They understand that if they don't do for themselves first, then it's liable not to happen at all. Start your mornings with the most important part of your day: you!

Listen here, sis: nothing is worth totally burning out because you haven't taken care of yourself. We must stop succumbing to the notion that those who don't take self-care breaks and are constantly busy are the real "hustlers." As I learned the hard way the day I received the call that my brother had died, sometimes it's more important to hit pause on the busyness of life and reconnect and recharge. Let's all let go of busy and live our best lives.

AGENT YOU:
TAKE ACTION!

1. Work smart, not hard. Sometimes we develop bad habits along the way to achieving our goals, even if we begin with good intentions.

   - Assess your daily tasks. Is there anything you've gotten into the habit of doing, even if it's unnecessary or time consuming? For instance, maybe you're a stay-at-home mom who also runs a business and spends hours meal planning, grocery shopping, doing meal prep, and so forth. Based on your budget, would it make more sense for you to order one or two meals a week from a delivery service so you can focus more time and energy on your family and your business?
   - Evaluate strategies you're using to reach your goals. Maybe, as I did when studying for my bar exam, you're spending time on completing a to-do list unnecessarily. Determine what's essential to reach your goal and focus on those activities.

2. Set priorities and say no first. These two go hand in hand—if you haven't set your priorities, you're more likely to say yes to anything and everything.

- Make a list of your priorities, the nonnegotiables in your world. Write down or type out this list and place it where you often engage in decision making (e.g., by your home computer, in your work cubicle, or in a note on your phone).
- Whenever you receive a request of any kind, say no first, then refer to your priorities list. Does the "ask" being made align with your priorities? If not, your no remains a no. If yes, make sure you're clear on why and how the ask fits in with your priorities and ensure that your boundaries are respected.

3. Set yourself as the top item on your daily to-do list. Don't let your self-care or personal needs get highjacked by a busy schedule. Every day, at the beginning of the day, make sure you do at least one thing that is for you and you alone, whether that's exercising, journaling, watching a TV show, emailing a good friend, and so forth.

Learn to let go of busy—glorifying the hustle is a one-way street to burnout.

CHAPTER THIRTEEN

Curate Your Tribe

am a movement by myself, but I'm even more powerful with my tribe. Let me be abundantly clear: your tribe will make or break you. In my journey to becoming a successful sports agent, I know how important my tribe is. As I sit here and type this book, one of my friends is working on an emergency graphic design for an impromptu meeting I just secured with an NBA player tomorrow; another friend is checking on me daily to ensure I've gotten sleep; one friend is stalking an NFL recruit for me on Instagram; and another friend is at the mall right now finding me something to wear to a speaking engagement, because I don't have the time.

In your journey to find purpose and peace, it's crucial that you have the right people surrounding you and pouring into your life.

As an agent, part of my job is ensuring that my athletes are surrounded by the right people. I make sure they have a trustworthy financial adviser, a savvy accountant, and a top-of-the-line publicist. All these people play a huge role in the success of an athlete's career. On the flip side, I also have to ensure the athlete doesn't surround himself (or herself) with people who will be detrimental to his success—family members who drain the athlete's bank accounts or friends who encourage the athlete to make faulty decisions.

As an agent of your own life, it's important to take an inventory of your tribe. Does your tribe contribute to your success? Does your tribe check on you to ensure your mental health is intact? Does your tribe let you know when you're wrong? Does your tribe push you to walk in your purpose while marching along with you? If not, sis—*clean up on aisle five*—it's time to get a new tribe!

BUILDING OUT YOUR TRIBE

Let's break down exactly what to look for when building out your tribe.

Adding Value

When I think of the number one requirement of being in my tribe, I think of how that person is adding value to my life. Many people would say, "Relationships shouldn't be about what someone can give or do for you." That is a flat-out lie.

We weren't placed in people's lives by accident. Our tribe isn't mended together coincidentally. Each and every person in your tribe has a purpose, and that purpose should add value to your life. The value could be that they give you a sense of peace when they're around. Or they help push you outside of your comfort zone. Or they're a listening ear when you need it most. Look at each person in your tribe and ask if they are a value add. Anyone not adding value to your life is not meant to be in your tribe. On the flip side, make sure you're equally adding value to your friendships. Relationships are a two-way street.

My Holy of Holies

Ever since I was a kid, I've used the term "my holy of holies" to define my closest friends: my day ones, my ride-or-dies, my besties. This group traditionally has been small. Barring a few exceptions, many of my holy of holies have been part of my tribe for an extended period. The members of this exclusive group know me on the deepest level. Honestly, they probably know me better than I know myself. For example, they could probably order my meal at a restaurant and get it right. They're the most likely to know exactly how I'll react in any number of situations. They know my biggest fears, they are aware of my insecurities, and they keep my biggest secrets. Even more important, my holy of holies keep me in check and know my weaknesses and help me push past them.

When you identify the members of your tribe, keep in mind that there are relationship levels. Just because someone is in your tribe doesn't mean they're in your holy of holies.

As you build bonds with people, be selective about who you let into your holy of holies. If someone is your friend or a work acquaintance, that doesn't mean they get access to the most personal parts of your life. For the people not in your holy of holies, they're either friends or social friends. Friends are people you share common interests with, people you can have fun with, and people who have your best interests in mind. They may not know your darkest secrets, but they do have a general pulse on your life and are provided more details than what you put on your highlight reel (i.e., social media). Social friends, on the other hand, are exactly that: people you see in social settings. You're friendly with social friends in public, and you likely come from some similar place or similar group of people (e.g., went to the same high school, attended a conference together, or is a friend of a friend), but they don't know any intimate details about your life. This group also includes people on social media that you haven't met in real life.

Here is an easy trick to help categorize your tribe members:

- Holy of holies stand next to you at your wedding.
- Friends are invited to your wedding.
- Social friends comment on your wedding pictures on social media.

Everyone Can't Come with You

Whew, child—somebody say it louder for the people in the back. Where you are going in life, everyone cannot come with you. Every relationship isn't meant to be forever. In fact, many relationships are only meant for a season. When God gives you a seasonal relationship with someone, keep it that way. It's okay to move these seasonal relationships, or relationships that weren't meant to come with you, into a different sphere of friendship. When you bring the wrong people with you on your journey, this can absolutely hinder your success. And let me nip this in the bud right now: just because you don't bring someone with you doesn't mean "you've changed" or "are too good." Instead, you are just fully aware of who God placed in your life to come along on your journey.

Be Around People Who Bring Out Your Best Self

Your tribe should include a diverse group of friends whose strengths don't necessarily match yours, but their strengths bring out your best self. In your tribe, maybe you have someone who is good at motivating you to push yourself further in your career. Maybe you have a friend who is into fitness and healthy eating and helps you in this area. Or it could be as simple as you knowing that your attitude, energy, and overall morale are better when they're around. We need people who bring out the side of us that we're most proud of people seeing. People who strengthen our weaknesses, who don't feed into our bad habits. Does your tribe do this?

The Energy Should Be Right

Although it may sound cliché, when choosing your tribe, the energy should feel right. You know that gut feeling you have when you know something is right, or when you can strongly feel something is off? It's your instinct—the little voice whispering in your head, or your discernment flashers blinking. If something doesn't feel right, it probably isn't.

People with Whom You Can Be Your True Self

I have a lot of quirks. For example, when eating at a restaurant, I don't like when people place their crumpled, used napkins on the table. I can't sleep alone in a house. I am afraid to fly. When you're with members of your tribe, you need to be comfortable as your true self, without covering. You should be willing to be vulnerable in front of them. You shouldn't feel the need to hide who you are—even the bad parts, weird quirks, and imperfections.

Birds of a Feather Flock Together

It's much more productive to have a diverse makeup of people in your tribe, whether different personalities or different upbringings. However, I do believe some common denominator usually draws people together. One of your close friends couldn't be more different than you, but I bet that, at your core, you two have a crucial similarity.

For instance, my husband is an integral part of my tribe, yet we couldn't be more different. I'm the life of the party, a talker who loves meeting strangers. He's an introvert and values and appreciates his small group of people. He loves to work out and is a former professional athlete. I hate working out and struggle to walk up the stairs without getting winded.

How do we make it work? Although we're polar opposites in many ways, when you peel back our layers, our cores align: our beliefs, our morals, our values, our outlook on life. Several factors draw us together. They say, tell me who your friends are and I can tell you who you are. I interpret this not to mean that you're the exact same as your friends and have similar personalities, but that there's something about your friends that could provide an outsider with a blueprint of you without even meeting you—that you and your friends align on what matters most.

Be Open to New Friendships

When I first started at my law firm, I was informed that another black girl around my age was starting at the same time.

This was a big deal because, in our 250-attorney office, we were the only black girls. I said to myself that I was almost thirty years old and, frankly, I wasn't interested in making new friends. I already had an amazing tribe that consisted of several decades-long friendships. Many of my tribe members and I had been together through hell and back over the years. I couldn't fathom the idea of adding new friends to my tribe and building a new relationship from scratch. Lucky for me, this girl was determined that we would be friends and, four years later, I can't imagine my life without her. She is an integral part of my tribe and has helped me get through some of my darkest days. Would you believe it when I say she is also in my holy of holies? She was my missing piece.

No matter your age or where you are in life, open yourself up for new relationships. Sometimes it could be the exact person you never knew you needed. This situation leads right into my next point . . .

Time Doesn't Dictate the Level or
Depth of the Friendship

If you've known someone your entire life, that doesn't mean the relationship is more or less important than the relationship with someone you met six months ago. We've all heard stories of a couple who dated for three months and have been married for thirty years, or a couple who dated for ten years and divorced after one year. Time isn't an indicator of anything. Don't justify or prioritize the friendships you've had longer. In that same vein, even if you talk to someone every day, that doesn't indicate closeness. We all have those friends we can go six to eight months without talking to, and it's like we never missed a beat. That person you can go long stints without talking to, but when you do, it refreshes your soul.

Don't Let Your Important Friendships Die

One attribute people often forget about when thinking of friends is forgiveness. When you have people who are close to you and woven into your life, they'll eventually hurt you, whether they do so intentionally or not. Prepare yourself for this and, in advance, decide which friendships you won't let die. Decide to forgive the people who have hurt you. Also, be willing to put in the hard work for your relationships. Sometimes, this means apologizing first or not indulging in giving someone the silent treatment or discovering the other person's love language and working to show your love in whatever method matters most to him or her. Some people love to receive gifts, others love to hear words of affirmation, some want to spend quality time with you, and so forth.

Move the Basket

In my first year of marriage, my husband drove me insane. We fought about everything. Communication, cleaning, finances—it was a never-ending battle.

One of my best friends had married the year before and was my go-to for newlywed advice. She told me that her husband would come home every day and drop his jeans right in front of the laundry basket. Not in the basket, but a foot in front of it, on the floor. She explained that they fought repeatedly about this small problem. Then one day, she had an *aha* moment: "I'm going to just move the basket," she said. She moved the basket to the place where he always dropped his jeans, and—wouldn't you know?—the jeans landed in the basket every day.

This story changed my life and all my relationships going forward. When working to keep important relationships, be willing to "move the basket." In other words, sometimes it takes *you* changing something or meeting someone halfway to get to the common goal. Think about how much easier it was for my friend to move the freaking basket instead of fighting over it every day.

Drop the pride and move the basket. I promise it will change your life.

AGENT YOU:
TAKE ACTION!

1. Make a list of everyone you consider part of your tribe.

    *   In what way(s) does each tribe member contribute value to your life?
    *   In what way(s) do you contribute value to the life of each member of your tribe?

2. Curate your tribe. Do you have anyone who is still part of your tribe, even though his or her purpose in your life has been fulfilled? For instance, maybe your best friend from college only seems to reach out to you when she needs something, and she never asks about your life and how you're doing. Or perhaps you have an old flame you message on social media or text, just in case your current relationship doesn't work out. Think about how you can gracefully either move these relationships into a different sphere of friendship or eliminate them from your life altogether.

3. Say thanks. What ways can you show appreciation
    to your tribe, especially those in your holy of
    holies? Keep in mind that people receive love in
    different ways. Can you write a note, describing
    the ways those friends add value to your life? Cook
    their favorite meal? Schedule a weekend
    adventure with them? Offer a night of babysitting,
    so they can have some personal time? If you're
    already practicing gratitude with your tribe
    members, keep up the great work.

Your tribe can make
or break you—choose
its members wisely.

CONCLUSION

When deciding on the foreword for this book, I immediately knew I wanted to ask Gabrielle Union. She is a cheerleader for equality who's dedicated to elevating women across the world. She's also her own best advocate and used to being the only woman in the room. Gabrielle gets it—she is her own agent.

I was well aware of Gabrielle's star power and how unlikely it was that she knew of me. Nevertheless, I decided that ask was still worth a try. If you've learned anything about me in this book, you know I'll always at least shoot my shot, even if I end up missing.

However, tracking down her contact information proved challenging (after all, you can't just google her phone number). My literary agent asked me to start thinking about my second choice, since we hadn't been able to reach Gabrielle. *Second choice?* I didn't have a second choice. As with pursuing my dream job as a sports agent, I didn't want to go to plan B. Gabrielle was always meant to write the foreword to this book.

Somehow, I'm going to get in contact with Gabrielle Union.

As I started to brainstorm, I decided that I'd try to get her to notice me on Twitter. A Hail Mary, if you will (pretty fitting for this book, huh?).

"Does anyone know of a way I can get in touch with Gabrielle Union?" I tweeted.

Ten minutes later, I received a DM, and to my surprise, it was from her! *Excuse me, is this Gabrielle Union in my DMs?* This wasn't a DM from someone connecting us or brainstorming with me on how to reach her. This was a DM from the woman herself. I just about lost it. Not in a million years did I expect her to message me. And, to top it off, she immediately agreed to write the foreword! I couldn't believe someone of her caliber agreed to write my foreword.

As I sat there reading the Twitter DM over and over again to ensure it was real, it hit me: *That moment, that tweet, that plan, that shot taken, is the epitome of being your own agent.*

I'm an agent for a lot of people, but in that moment, I got to experience exactly what it feels like to be my own agent. To step out on a limb, to take the jump, to advocate for myself, and to shoot my shot.

●　●　●

If you take only one thing from this entire book, I want you to remember this: *You have a purpose for being on this earth—you were not placed here by accident.*

No matter how long it takes or how many hurdles you have to jump, find that purpose and walk in it every single day. And when you find purpose, do every single thing you can to find and protect your peace. Purpose and peace will change your entire life.

Thank you for reading this. I hope this book has encouraged you to let go of fear and to believe in yourself. To chase your dreams, but to do so with a plan and with intention. To work harder than your peers but also take care of yourself along the way. To not take no for an answer. To be your authentic self every single place you go, while remembering that *you* are the secret sauce. To give yourself grace and to remember that you are doing the best you can. And, most important, to be your own agent.

APPENDIX A

Agent You: Take Action! Exercises

CHAPTER ONE:
FIND YOUR PURPOSE

1. Use the steps provided in this chapter to identify your purpose. Make a list of four or five things you're really good at, then cross off any item that doesn't meet the following criteria:

   * Things you truly enjoy;
   * Things that impact the world; and
   * Things you would do for free, if money were no object.

   After this process, you should only have one, perhaps two, items on your list.

   _____

   _____

   _____

_____

_____

2. Find a way to walk in your purpose. If you're already living out your purpose, congratulations! However, if you aren't, you may need to find the time and energy to make this a reality. Think of at least one or two ways, small or large, that enable you to start walking in your purpose *today*.

_____

_____

3. Begin planning for the long term. Even if you have other commitments keeping you from walking fully in your purpose right now, it's never too late to start planning for the future. In a journal, a note on your phone, or a document on your computer, start envisioning how your day-to-day life will look when you're walking in your purpose. Think about not only the practical elements, but the positive mental and emotional benefits that walking in your purpose will have on you.

CHAPTER TWO:
GET YOUR DREAM JOB

1. Make a list of five small things you can do to work toward your dream job.

- If you need to schedule time each day to hold yourself accountable for completing these tasks, do so. Also, remember to include easy tasks on your list, for the days you have less time or motivation.
- When you complete this first list, start a new one—keep the momentum going.

_____

_____

_____

_____

_____

_____

_____

_____

_____

2. Think of at least five people you can ask for a ten-to-fifteen-minute commitment to have a phone conversation or grab coffee. After you do this, brainstorm ideas around the answers to the following questions:

- How can you get in front of these people? Do you share any mutual connections? Can you direct message (DM) them on social media? Are they attending an event you can gain entrance to?
- How can you demonstrate added value to each person on your list? Can you make a connection for them? Do you have a skill that these people or their organizations are lacking?

_____

_____

_____

_____

_____

3. Though it's not possible for everyone, consider working for experience.

   - How many hours a week could you commit to this undertaking? Setting limits from the outset will help keep you from being taken advantage of.
   - Document everything you gain from this experience: build a portfolio, list your accomplishments on your résumé, and so forth.
   - If you absolutely can't work solely to gain experience, consider bartering your services. Is there someone who needs a service you can offer who also can provide you with a service?

CHAPTER THREE:
BE YOUR AUTHENTIC SELF

_____

1. Your "me statement" is a critical part of being your authentic self. This statement covers five areas: identity, belief, stance, enjoyment, and legacy. To assess each of these areas, ask yourself the following questions:

- Identity: How do you view yourself? List the primary ways.

  _____

  _____

- Belief: What are your core values? If you're struggling to come up with ideas, an online search will point you toward dozens of websites that provides lists you can choose from.

  _____

  _____

- Stance: What cause would you march in the streets to support? Even if you'd support multiple causes in this way, if you could only choose one, what would it be?

  _____

  _____

- Enjoyment: What activities make you happy? If you're like me and have trouble pinpointing things you enjoy, try to remember times when you've smiled and laughed a lot, and what you were doing then.

  _____

  _____

- Legacy: If you could choose one thing for people to remember about you after you die, what would it be? Keep in mind that this can be something close to home, such as "I want people to remember that I loved my family," or something broader, such as "I want people to remember that I fought for global women's rights to education."

_____

_____

CHAPTER FOUR:
TREAT YOURSELF LIKE THE BRAND YOU ARE

1. Ask yourself: "How do I envision my brand?" One helpful way to answer this question is to fill in the blank. For instance, I am Agent Nicole Lynn: my brand and my name. Who do you want to be known as?

_____

_____

2. Take steps to build your brand. Even if you've already begun the process of building your brand, now is a good time to evaluate the work you've already done and make sure you haven't gotten off track along the way.

- Choose your pillars. What do you want people to think of when they think of you?
- Choose your theme. What do you want people to think of when they think of your brand?
- Identify your audience. Who is your brand intended to reach and help?
- Choose your medium. Where are you most likely to engage your audience?
- Be consistent. Across all your platforms, make sure that all the content relates to at least one of your pillars, adheres to your theme, will appeal to your audience, and is appropriate for the medium.

3. Make every effort not to cover. Most of us fall victim to covering in one way or another, whether in the workplace or elsewhere. Evaluate the things about yourself or your life that you've withheld from others. Are you keeping those things under wraps because of fear or a desire to make sure others are comfortable? If you're covering in any way, you can begin by writing down one thing and listing at least two or three ways you, those around you, or those who come after you can benefit from your refusal to cover.

_____

_____

_____

_____

CHAPTER FIVE:
EMBRACE A MAMBA MENTALITY

1. Keep in mind that success isn't always pretty. You most likely have what it takes to succeed, but are you willing to do what it takes to succeed?

    - What are you willing to sacrifice to achieve your desired success? A long-term relationship? Financial security? Sleep?
    - What are you unwilling to sacrifice? These are your nonnegotiables, which can help you eliminate options along your journey to success. Sometimes it's equally important to know what you *aren't* willing to do as it is to know what you are willing to do.

2. Use what you have. We all have finite resources, and some of us have access to more resources than others.

    - Make a list of the things you think you need to succeed (e.g., more time, a degree, a part-time assistant).

    _____

    _____

    - Do you currently have all these resources? If not, how can you secure them? Or do you already have something that can serve as a substitute for the time being? For instance, if you need more time but can't afford childcare, maybe you could offer one of your skills in exchange for a friend watching your kid(s) for a few hours a week.

3. Define success on your terms. Complete this sentence: I consider success to be _____.

CHAPTER SIX:
STAY READY, SO YOU
DON'T HAVE TO GET READY

1. Reflect on times when fear prevented you from taking your shot.

- Has fear ever prevented you from pursuing your dream? If so, what do you wish you'd done differently, or what can you start doing differently right now (e.g., not indulge in self-defeatist thought patterns, such as, *No one's ever going to take me seriously, so why should I even bother?*)?

  _____

  _____

  _____

- Have you ever taken your shot in spite of your fear? If so, how were you able to accomplish this?

And how can you remind yourself of this victory the next time fear threatens to paralyze you? For instance, can you make a list of victories to revisit any time you feel afraid or insecure?

_____

_____

_____

2. How can you *stay ready*, right now? In this chapter, I listed several ways you can stay ready. Make a list of three tasks you can work on today so you're prepared when opportunity comes your way. If you're unsure of what you can or should do to prepare, consult a trusted friend or mentor or ask someone who works in the industry.

_____

_____

_____

CHAPTER SEVEN:
GET COMFORTABLE WITH LOSING

1. Use affirmations to focus, stay positive, and keep your emotions in check. Mentally prepare yourself for failure, so you're not derailed when it happens.

• If you know and admire someone successful, research that person's backstory. Did he or she experience losses before winning? If so, how were those challenges navigated? How can you use that story to keep you motivated?

- Transform your "what if" worst-case scenarios to "what if" best-case scenarios. For instance, instead of saying, "What if no one attends my grand-opening event?" say, "What if so many people attend my grand-opening event that it's standing room only, and the line wraps around the block?"
- Make a list of at least three positive outlets for the emotions you experience when you lose, then remind yourself of them. For example, "If I get turned down for the promotion, I will treat myself to a spa day, then ask my supervisor what I can do to put myself in a better position for the next promotion."

---

2. When you lose, consider that an opportunity to add skills to your toolbox. What did you learn from the experience that can set you up for success next time?

---

3. Count *all* your wins. It's easy to allow disappointment to cloud our vision instead of acknowledging even the small victories. In what ways, small or big, did

you win on your journey, even if a particular effort didn't succeed? Write down at least three things you can celebrate as wins.

_____

_____

_____

CHAPTER EIGHT:
DO ALL YOU CAN, THEN DO NO MORE

1. Think about this idea: "Even if you wanted to do more, you could not."

   • Are there any areas of your life where you simply cannot do more? Perhaps you've put in an insane number of hours at work, sacrificing your relationships and health, yet still haven't made partner. Or maybe you've tried everything you can think of to salvage a relationship, yet no improvement is being made.
   • Write down at least one area in your life that you have done all you could and need to let go and let God.

   _____

   _____

2. Consider an area or areas in your life where you're already trusting God, regardless of the outcome.

- One way to further commit to trusting him in that situation is to complete the following sentence: "I'm believing God for _____, but even if he doesn't, I'll still honor and worship him."

3. Another way to trust God with the outcome is to reflect on times when his answer to your prayer was no.

- List at least three times in your life you're grateful that God said no instead of yes.

_____

_____

_____

- How do those situations help you appreciate God's plan for your life?

CHAPTER NINE:
DITCH IMPOSTER SYNDROME

1. Check your tribe. Surround yourself with people who believe in you even when you don't believe in yourself.

- Who is the one person you can always count on to cheer you on but also tell it to you straight?
- Who are the five people who consistently call/ text/email you supportive and encouraging words?

- Who, after spending time with them, fills you up and makes you feel ready to take on the world?

_____

_____

_____

_____

_____

_____

_____

_____

_____

2. Don't just be prepared—be overprepared. Leave nothing on the table, and always be ready and willing to go above and beyond.

- What do you know you could be doing more of, more often, to overprepare? Make a list of three ways you can overprepare for a current project.

_____

_____

_____

3. Compare yourself to others. However, make sure you compare yourself to your peers, not those who are further down the path than you.

- Who has a similar education/experience level to you?

_____

_____

- If you have peers ahead of you on the path, what must you do to catch up to them?

CHAPTER TEN:
SCORE A SEAT AT THE TABLE

1. Get a seat at the table, _now_. Remember the five ways to secure your place:

   - _Keep your eyes open and research._ Who is at the table, and how did they get there? What can you learn from their journey that benefits you?
   - _Create a road map._ Make a list of your career goals and how you will achieve them. Think beyond salary to what all aspects of success look like for you.
   - _Stay aware._ Pay attention to how you're being treated, especially in relation to peers with the same level of experience as you.
   - _Advocate._ This is threefold: (1) Get comfortable asking uncomfortable questions. (2) Speak up about desiring more difficult assignments. (3) Document unconscious bias.

2. Choose a mentor. Recall the three criteria for a mentor, who should be (1) more experienced than you; (2) someone you trust; and (3) an adviser.

- Make a list of at least five people you think could mentor you.

_____

_____

_____

_____

- What specific benefits would each person bring to the relationship? For example, do they possess a skill set you want or need to learn to advance in your career? Or have they excelled in their career while also maintaining a healthy work-life balance?
- To narrow down your selection, you might also find it helpful to make a list of pros and cons for each person on the list.

3. Find a sponsor. You become someone's protégé because that person can advocate for you and leverage connections to get you where you want to go.

- List at least five potential sponsors.

_____

_____

_____

_____

- As with your mentors list, identify what specific benefits each person would bring to the relationship. Are they respected and admired by many people both inside and outside of your company? Do they have connections to clients or industry insiders who could greatly boost your career?
- Also similar to your mentor search, you can list pros and cons for each person on your potential sponsor list.
- If you can't find a sponsor right away, sponsor yourself! Keep a work journal where you record all your accomplishments, and practice showing instead of telling when you promote yourself.

CHAPTER ELEVEN:
PRACTICE SELF-CARE

1. Be okay with doing nothing. You can't start your self-care journey with actions. Begin by being. This doesn't come naturally to many people, but keep practicing.

2. Practice self-care. Self-care looks different for everyone, and it might take time for you to find activities that work for you.

   - Make a list of at least five ways you can practice daily self-care.

_____

_____

_____

_____

_____

- Now, list several ways you can practice weekly or monthly self-care.

_____

_____

_____

_____

_____

- Journal your self-care experiences, to hold yourself accountable and to ensure that your self-care activities don't feel like another item you have to check off your to-do list.

3. Protect your self-care time. Life will continually take from you, so if you don't fiercely guard your self-care sessions, something will consume that time.

 - After you've identified ways you can practice self-care, block off the necessary time on your calendar, and make these appointments with yourself nonnegotiable.
 - Don't be afraid to communicate these boundaries to others. If they respect you, they'll respect your self-care boundaries.

CHAPTER TWELVE:
LET GO OF BUSY

1. Work smart, not hard. Sometimes we develop bad habits along the way to achieving our goals, even if we begin with good intentions.

   - Assess your daily tasks. Is there anything you've gotten into the habit of doing, even if it's unnecessary or time consuming? For instance, maybe you're a stay-at-home mom who also runs a business and spends hours meal planning, grocery shopping, doing meal prep, and so forth. Based on your budget, would it make more sense for you to order one or two meals a week from a delivery service so you can focus more time and energy on your family and your business?
   - Evaluate strategies you're using to reach your goals. Maybe, as I did when studying for my bar exam, you're spending time on completing a to-do list unnecessarily. Determine what's essential to reach your goal and focus on those activities.

2. Set priorities and say no first. These two go hand in hand—if you haven't set your priorities, you're more likely to say yes to anything and everything.

- Make a list of your priorities, the nonnegotiables in your world. Write down or type out this list and place it where you often engage in decision making (e.g., by your home computer, in your work cubicle, or in a note on your phone).
- Whenever you receive a request of any kind, say no first, then refer to your priorities list. Does the "ask" being made align with your priorities? If not, your no remains a no. If yes, make sure you're clear on why and how the ask fits in with your priorities and ensure that your boundaries are respected.

3. Set yourself as the top item on your daily to-do list. Don't let your self-care or personal needs get highjacked by a busy schedule. Every day, at the beginning of the day, make sure you do at least one thing that is for you and you alone, whether that's exercising, journaling, watching a TV show, emailing a good friend, and so forth.

CHAPTER THIRTEEN: CURATE YOUR TRIBE

1. Make a list of everyone you consider part of your tribe.

- In what way(s) does each tribe member contribute value to your life?

- In what way(s) do you contribute value to the
  life of each member of your tribe?

_____

_____

_____

_____

_____

_____

_____

_____

_____

2. Curate your tribe. Do you have anyone who is still
   part of your tribe, even though his or her purpose
   in your life has been fulfilled? For instance, maybe
   your best friend from college only seems to reach
   out to you when she needs something, and she
   never asks about your life and how you're doing.
   Or perhaps you have an old flame you message on
   social media or text, just in case your current
   relationship doesn't work out. Think about how
   you can gracefully either move these relationships
   into a different sphere of friendship or eliminate
   them from your life altogether.

3. Say thanks. What ways can you show appreciation
   to your tribe, especially those in your holy of
   holies? Keep in mind that people receive love in
   different ways. Can you write a note describing the

ways those friends add value to your life? Cook
their favorite meal? Schedule a weekend
adventure with them? Offer a night of babysitting,
so they can have some personal time? If you're
already practicing gratitude with your tribe
members, keep up the great work.

APPENDIX B

Things to Remember

- Everyone has a purpose—including you!
- *Today* is the day to start working toward your dream job.
- You—and only you—determine your authentic self.
- No matter who you are, you are a brand.
- Only you can define what success looks like for *you*.
- *Stay* ready, so you don't have to *get* ready.
- You will lose, but you win when you keep going.
- When you let go and let God, you also trust him with the outcome.
- When you're true to yourself, you'll become more confident and overcome imposter syndrome.
- Don't wait—fight for your seat at the table today.
- Self-care is a priority, not a reward.
- Learn to let go of busy—glorifying the hustle is a one-way street to burnout.
- Your tribe can make or break you—choose its members wisely.

ACKNOWLEDGMENTS

Where do I even begin?

This book, my career, and everything you see in *Agent You* would not be possible—*is* not possible—without my husband, Gabe. You are my entire world. Thank you for supporting every one of my dreams. You are such an important part of not only this book, but my story. My story ends differently without you. I'm crying as I write this, because no one will ever know just how amazing you are. Thank you for your love and support throughout this journey.

To my parents. Mom, you are the sweetest, most kind person who has ever walked this planet. Life hasn't always been easy for you, but you would never let the world know it. Your smile is contagious, and your joy is a goal that only few will ever achieve. Thank you for teaching me at a young age how to love Jesus. My faith in God is what has gotten me to this place. Growing up, you didn't have any tangible items to give me, but what you *could* give me matters most. You taught me how to love people like Christ loves them. You taught me how to worship God and lean on him through it all.

Dad, thank you for doing the best you could with the little you had, and for the work ethic and desire to learn that you instilled in me. I love you greatly.

To my in-laws, Ronda and Tyrone. Thank you for accepting me into your family and loving me just the same. I am beyond blessed to have a bonus mom and dad who truly see me as a daughter. And most importantly, thank you for raising such an amazing son.

And to Martin, thank you for loving my mom every single day. We are so glad we have you in our family.

To my brother, Julius. I am so proud of you and all that you have accomplished! You are not, and will never be, a product of your circumstances. You've worked so hard, and your time is coming. And thank you to Boo, Ijeoma, Vanessa, Valencia, Avani, T.J., and Cooda Jr. (may he rest in peace).

To my friends, beginning with Taylor Hornsby. There aren't enough pages in this book for all the words I want to write. Thank you for being "my person" for more than half my life. I wouldn't be where I am today without you, my best friend, standing by my side through it all. I love you to life!

To Taylor Moore and Lauren Vickers, the friends I never knew I needed. I can't thank God enough for ensuring that we would become friends. Taylor, thank you for letting me include your very personal story in this book with the hopes that it will resonate with someone on the deepest level. I love watching you be a mom, and I already love baby Faith so much. Thank you for reading and editing pages upon pages of this book for me and encouraging me to include personal stories (even those I sometimes forgot, maybe intentionally). This book would not have been possible without you.

To Christine, for getting me through my darkest moments in my life while still having to move your own personal mountains. For always loving me, despite my faults. For being the person I know I can depend on for anything, at any time. I don't say this lightly: I trust you with my life.

To Crystal. I wouldn't have made it this far without you. Thank you for always taking on my journey as if it were your own. And for laughing at every single one of my jokes and being the exact replica of me. And for being my biggest and loudest cheerleader. Everyone needs a Crystal.

To the dream team, Amelia, Kim, and Mitcham, for believing in me back in our first year of law school even when others didn't. To my entire tribe—Kim Kelly, Lauren McMillan, Thomas Glenn, Jordan Nelson, and my line sisters (D-16)—thank you!

To Boog and Ray, the big brothers I never had and behind-the-scenes heroes.

To Teri Shaw ("Sis"). It was the honor of a lifetime to know you. I wish we could have done more. Thank you for teaching me to help others the way they want to be helped. I love and miss you more than you will ever know. "It's just me, you, and Gabe." RIP.

To the best literary agent in the game, Shannon. Thank you believing that my story needed to be heard. When we sat down for lunch in New York City and talked about goals and dreams, I knew it was always supposed to be you. From one agent to another, I am so grateful for you and couldn't have made it through this process without you.

To Harper Horizon. Andrea, when we met in New York City, Shannon and I had just wrapped up several publisher interviews. Five minutes into our conversation, I knew I wanted to work with you and your team. I immediately told Shannon that I'd finish out the rest of the interviews, but Andrea was the one. I haven't regretted that decision one day since. Thank you for taking a chance on a first-time author when the pressure was already high, with you leading a new imprint. To Amanda, thank you for turning water into wine while editing my pages. It gave me so much solace in knowing that we had similar upbringings, and when reading my stories and the words on the pages, you just got it. Thank you for all of your words of wisdom; they have been needed! To John and the rest of the Harper team, thank you for everything you've contributed to this book's success.

To my clients, thank you for believing in me and choosing me to navigate your career. I don't take it for granted and am grateful every single day.

To Gabrielle Union, thank you for agreeing to write the foreword for this book—and for showing me and other women what it means to be your own agent.

To Ken Sarnoff, thank you for taking a chance on a young agent when no one else would. I am forever grateful for you.

And last but not least, I want to thank God for protecting me all of these years, for his grace and mercy that I do not deserve, and for his favor on my life.

NOTES

CHAPTER TWO

1. Jerry Rice (@JerryRice), posted to Twitter, February 25, 2015, https:// twitter.com/JerryRice/status/570623680755175424.
2. Nathaniel Bastin, "In the Beginning: Legendary Origin Stories of Amazon, Microsoft, Apple and 7 More," The Startup, Medium.com, October 13, 2020, https://medium.com/swlh/in-the-beginning-legendary -origin-stories-of-amazon-microsoft-apple-and-7-more-a7224e42628a.
3. Marguerite Ward, "8 Business Icons Who Found Success After Age 40," CNBC, February 9, 2017, https://www.cnbc.com/2017/02/09/8 -business-icons-who-found-success-after-age-40.html.

CHAPTER THREE

1. Lin-Manuel Miranda, *Hamilton: The Revolution,* ed. Jeremy McCarter (New York: Grand Central Publishing, 2016).

CHAPTER FOUR

1. Julie Rafferty, "'Covering' to Fit In and Get Ahead," Harvard T. H. Chan School of Public Health, August 26, 2015, https://www.hsph .harvard.edu/news/features/covering-to-fit-in-and-get-ahead/.
2. Matt Thompson, "Five Reasons Why People Code-Switch," NRP.org, April 13, 2013, https://www.npr.org/sections/codeswitch/2013/04 /13/177126294/five-reasons-why-people-code-switch.

CHAPTER FIVE

1. Claire Bradley, "7 Millionaire Myths," Investopedia, March 17, 2020, https://www.investopedia.com/financial-edge/0810/7-millionaire

-myths.aspx#:~:text=It's%20a%20myth%20that%20millionaires
,about%2080%25%20worked%20for%20it.

2. Jennifer Cohen, "The Difference Between People Who Succeed and People Who Flop," *Forbes,* July 27, 2018, https://www.forbes.com/sites/ jennifercohen/2018/07/27/the-difference-between-people -who-succeed-and-people-who-flop/?sh=e05e59071831.

CHAPTER SEVEN

1. Rachel Gillett, "How Walt Disney, Oprah Winfrey, and 19 Other Successful People Rebounded After Getting Fired," *Inc.,* October 7, 2015.
2. Recording Industry Association of America, "Gold & Platinum," accessed February 23, 2021, https://www.riaa.com/gold-platinum/?tab _active=default-award&ar=Beyonce&ti=Dangerously+in+Love#search _section.

CHAPTER NINE

1. Megan Dalla-Camina, "The Reality of Imposter Syndrome," *Psychology Today,* September 3, 2018, https://www.psychologytoday.com/us /blog/real-women/201809/the-reality-imposter-syndrome.

CHAPTER TEN

1. Rachel Thomas et al., *Women in the Workplace 2020,* McKinsey & Company and LeanIn.Org, September 2020, https://wiw-report.s3.amazon aws.com/Women_in_the_Workplace_2020.pdf.
2. Zhiyu Feng et al., "Research: A Method for Overcoming Implicit Bias When Considering Job Candidates," *Harvard Business Review,* July 21, 2020, https://hbr.org/2020/07/research-a-method-for-overcoming -implicit-bias-when-considering-job-candidates.
3. Vivian Giang, "7 Successful Women Explain How They Got the Sponsor That Changed Their Careers," *Fast Company,* February 26, 2019, https://www.fastcompany.com/90307513/7-successful-women-explain -how-they-got-the-sponsor-that-changed-their-careers; Sylvia Ann Hewlett, "The Right Way to Find a Career Sponsor," *Harvard Business Review,* September 11, 2013, https://hbr.org/2013/09/the-right-way-to -find-a-career-sponsor.
4. Ivie Temitayo-Ibitoye, "Ivie Temitayo-Ibitoye: The Differeence Between Sponsors & Mentors," *Bella Naija,* March 16, 2020, https://www .bellanaija.com/2020/03/ivie-temitayo-ibitoye-the-difference-between -sponsors-mentors/.
5. Rachel Thomas, et al., *Women in the Workplace 2020,* McKinsey & Company and LeanIn.Org, September 2020, https://wiw-report.s3.amazon aws.com/Women_in_the_Workplace_2020.pdf.

CHAPTER ELEVEN

1. Brené Brown, "Brené Brown: Why Goofing Off Is Really Good for You," *HuffPost,* December 6, 2017, https://www.huffpost.com/entry /brene-brown-importance-of-play_n_4675625.

ABOUT THE AUTHOR

Nicole Lynn is an attorney and former Wall Street analyst. After becoming an NFL agent, she signed her first major player within three months on the job at just twenty-six years old. Today, Nicole has a dual career as an attorney with one of the world's largest law firms while also working as an elite agent to professional athletes, broadcasters, and entertainers. In 2019, Nicole became the first black woman to represent a top 3 NFL draft pick.

Nicole has been named one of the most powerful women in sports by *Sports Illustrated* and was recognized on *Glamour* magazine's "Women of the Year" list for her pioneering success as an NFL agent. A new TV show inspired by Nicole's life and career will be produced and released by Curtis "50 Cent" Jackson and STARZ.